R EFERENCE G UIDES IN L ITERATURE
N UMBER 12
Everett Emerson, *Editor*
Joseph Katz, *Consulting Editor*

John and William Bartram, William Byrd II and St. John de Crèvecoeur: *A Reference Guide*

Rose Marie Cutting

G. K. HALL & CO., 70 LINCOLN STREET, BOSTON, MASS.

Library of Congress Cataloging in Publication Data

Cutting, Rose Marie.
   John and William Bartram, William Byrd II, and
St. John de Crèvecoeur.

   (Reference guides in literature ; no. 12)
   Includes index.
   1. Bartram, John, 1699-1777--Bibliography.
2. Bartram, William, 1739-1823--Bibliography.
3. Byrd, William, 1674-1744--Bibliography.
4. Crèvecœur, Michel Guillaume St. Jean de, called
Saint John de Crèvecœur, 1735-1813--Bibliography.
Z1231.P8C87   [PS362]   016.808   76-2501
ISBN 0-8161-1176-6

This publication is printed on permanent/durable acid-free paper.
MANUFACTURED IN THE UNITED STATES OF AMERICA

Contents

Introduction

Interest in John Bartram has been sustained on three bases: his work as scientist, his achievement in founding the Bartram botanical garden, and his character as a model American. Bartram's unadorned writing style has excited little critical notice.

I. Botanist

By the middle of the eighteenth century, John Bartram's work was being highly praised by his fellow scientists. Peter Kalm, a Swedish naturalist and pupil of Linnaeus, visited Bartram in 1748, and in his Travels into North America (1770) praised Bartram's acute powers of observation, "great knowledge," and many discoveries in the field of botany. Linnaeus himself called the self-taught scientist "the greatest natural botanist in the world." Crèvecoeur, undoubtedly Bartram's most effective publicist, described a (probably fictional) visit to Bartram by a Russian in Letters from an American Farmer (1782). The Russian enthusiastically lauds the first botanist to bring "honour to America," and endows Bartram with "general knowledge of every plant and tree on the continent."

In 1804, William Bartram published a biographical tribute to his late father, surveying John Bartram's botanical work, declaring he "seemed to be designed for the study and contemplation of nature," and calling him probably the first Anglo-American to establish a botanical garden (though there were earlier botanical gardens in North America). William Bartram's biographical sketch and Crèvecoeur's essay were reprinted in William Darlington's 1849 volume Memorials of John Bartram and Humphry Marshall, a collection of Bartram's correspondence which is the chief primary source of material on the man and his work. Most succeeding publications on Bartram have been based on it. Thus Darlington insured that William Bartram's and Crèvecoeur's accounts would continue to be quoted and paraphrased during the nineteenth and twentieth centuries.

Paraphrasers, including Darlington himself, have stretched Bartram's reputation by distorting his son's careful wording.

Darlington's prefatory remarks on "Progress of Botany in North America," for example, rather cautiously cite John Bartram as probably the first to start a botanical garden in British America; but a few pages later, in a biographical sketch, Darlington glorifies his subject as "the earliest native American Botanist, and the founder of the first Botanical Garden on this continent"--neat epithets which had already found acceptance before the publication of Memorials.

Bartram's correspondence was extensive, especially his interchange with the British gardener Peter Collinson, who first encouraged him to export American specimens. Scholars have drawn on the Bartram correspondence for their discussions of Bartram's relationships and scientific exchanges with European and American gardeners and scientists, the honor and praise these people accorded him, his travels to discover and collect American flora, the shipment of American plants and seeds to England, the Bartram Garden as nursery for American and foreign plants, and Bartram's scientific experiments.

Articles on Bartram provide discussions of his work in other sciences (geography, geology, anthropology), of the joint discovery by John and William Bartram of the "Franklin tree," and of the southern routes the pair traveled. The Bartram travel journals constitute a second major primary source of data.

II. Bartram Garden

Many discussions of John Bartram note the importance of the Bartram Garden in international horticultural exchange. Seeds and plants from the twelve-acre plot outside Philadelphia were exported to stock the gardens of England. The centennial of the garden's founding, 1831, marks the beginning of a steady series of publications on the garden itself, which continued through the bicentennial. The purchase of the garden for a city park in 1889, and the subsequent restoration of the garden and the house, contributed to public interest. The stone house, built by John Bartram with his own hands, has drawn attention for both its architectural and its historic significance.

III. Character: John Bartram's Mythic Stature

The life of John Bartram seems to exemplify a number of important ideals. Combining, as do Darlington and his successors, the characterizations by Crèvecoeur and William Bartram, we get a picture of a simple, self-educated farmer who surmounted all difficulties to achieve eminence; a model of piety and independence who was zealous against slavery and freed his own slaves; a distinguished scientist, honored by luminaries of two continents, who continued to live in Quaker simplicity on the model farm he had created--though his stubborn independence had earned him disownment by the Quakers.

Some commentators view this glowing picture of the man more critically than others, notably Wilson (1968), who complains that Bartram's artlessness has been overemphasized in order to contrast him with the artistic William. But even Wilson concedes that the Bartram "fiction . . . may be treated as valid in general outline." We have little source material that in any way contradicts the myth of the model citizen.

Bartram's character is as important to his reputation as his scientific achievements. Linnaeus's description of Bartram as the "greatest natural botanist" of his age shows the eighteenth-century appreciation for primitive genius, and the remark is echoed in Allibone's dictionary (1859), the National Cyclopedia of Biography (1897), and the Dictionary of American Biography (1929). Bartram's lack of formal training is the recurrent fillip to his reputation as scientist.

It was Crèvecoeur who first brought together all the elements of the Bartram myth and gave it a literary form. Crèvecoeur, casting Bartram as the archetypal American convert, likewise first told the tale most often repeated by others: John Bartram once paused in his ploughing to observe, with uncommon curiosity, a common daisy, and from that moment on was "inspired" to study nature.

IV. Writings

Introducing the diary of Bartram's southern journey, Francis Harper declares that the work has "scarcely a single literary flourish," but provides a valuable picture of the American wilderness. From the earliest comments in 1751 up to the present, Bartram's writings have been described as "plain," "the barest statement of fact," and "rather labored," but nevertheless valuable. At most, there are only "fragments which so wed content and style as to qualify as art."

In addition to his correspondence, John Bartram's chief writings consist of two travel journals--one of a northern trip to an Iroquois council, Observations (1751); and the Diary of a Journey through the Carolinas, Georgia, and Florida, 1765-66 (1944), partially published in 1767. The journals and letters supply important materials on botanical history and America's largely untouched and unexplored natural resources, and furnish a picture of cultural and scientific thought in eighteenth-century America.

WILLIAM BARTRAM (1739-1823)

On his journey through what was to become the Southern states, John Bartram was accompanied by his son William Bartram. Eight years later, in 1773, William Bartram returned to retrace the same route, and out of his experiences composed his magnum opus,

Introduction

Travels through North & South Carolina, Georgia, East & West Florida
... (1791). The fountains and springs, violent storms, sunsets,
herons, ephemera, alligators, palm trees, magnolias, and wild straw-
berries of the Southeast, and the culture of the Indians who lived
there, were viewed by William Bartram with the eyes of the scientist,
the poet, and the artist. Travels is both a monument to the zest in
scientific exploration Bartram shared with his father, and a classic
of early American literature.

I. Scientist

In the eighteenth century, William Bartram's Travels was reprinted and translated in Europe an extraordinary number of times
(first edition, Philadelphia, 1791; two London editions, 1792, 1794;
a Dublin edition, 1793; a Berlin edition, 1793; an edition in Vienna,
1793; one or two Dutch editions, 1794, 1797; two French editions,
1799, 1801), but the book was seldom reviewed in contemporary journals. The reviews that were published, as well as the introductions
to foreign translations, indicate that Travels was valued largely
for its information on natural history and the American South. The
elaborate literary setting of the data is generally reviled by early
reviewers. One reviewer calls the style "very incorrect and dis-
gustingly pompous" (1792); milder judgments include "rather too
luxuriant and florid" (1792) and "somewhat too luxuriant and poetical" (1793). The German translator Zimmerman "improved" Bartram by
pruning his supposed verbosity and bombast. Even the English editions of Travels were edited to tame Bartram's blend of poetry and
science.

Bartram's literary flourishes appear to have partially ob-
scured his contributions to science. Bartram was the first to name
many American plants and birds. Because his names and descriptions
are buried among his reflections in Travels and in his diary, however, nomenclature proposed by later workers became established before his achievements were brought to the attention of the scientific community. In the 1870s, Coues claimed priority for Bartram's
avian taxonomy in an extended published debate with Allen. Merrill
revived the subject again in 1945, claiming "merely because they
have been overlooked for a century and a half is no argument" against
Bartram's binomials being listed. Battles have been waged over the
correctness of Bartram's nomenclature, the adequacy of his descriptions, and the crucial question of where scientific accuracy may
have been cast aside in favor of poetic rapture.

His scientific accomplishments have been strongly defended
in the twentieth century, particularly by Harper, a consistent champion of Bartram as scientist. Ewan's introduction to Bartram's drawings (1968) conveys a sense of the broad range of Bartram's studies
as naturalist. A number of writers applaud Bartram's work on Indians
as a valuable contribution to anthropology and ethnology. Most con-
clude that Bartram was influenced by the cult of the noble savage,

but recorded Indian behavior and culture with scientific care and
literary realism.

II. Writer

During the nineteenth century, Travels began to attract
favorable notice as literature and to have a powerful influence on
other writers. Carlyle praised it highly; the Duyckincks, Allibone,
Lippincott and Tuckerman lauded the book for its descriptions of
nature, and the Duyckincks and Tuckerman paid tribute to its style.
Coleridge merely praised the book in passing in 1836, but he incor-
porated its pictures of America into his writings.

Bartram's influence on other writers has been a major subject of critical interest. Early in the twentieth century, the influence on Coleridge, Chateaubriand, and the Wordsworths was scru-
tinized. Fagin (1933) summarized and extended previous comments and
discussed Bartram's influence on a host of other English and American
writers who responded to the delights of Travels--Lamb, Shelley,
Carlyle, Emerson, Thoreau, Chivers, and Hearn.

Twentieth-century scholars have also investigated Bartram
from a thematic standpoint. His primitivism--a preference for the
primitive over the civilized, his depiction of the return to nature
as a return to Eden, his noble happy Indians--and his sense of the
immanence of the divine in the living, harmonious and unified organism which is nature--have come in for particular attention.

Several twentieth-century writers call attention to Travels
as a book that has suffered undeserved neglect; but even while the
neglect was being lamented, it was being rectified. Far more attention has been given to William Bartram, both as scientist and as
writer, in the present century than in the preceding two centuries.
Though modern critics admit Bartram occasionally goes too far in
exuberance and in combining the functions of scientist and poet, it
is Bartram's style which now excites more interest than any other
facet of his work, and eighteenth-century disdain has given way to
twentieth-century enthusiasm. Travels is a "narrative of infinite
riches and variety" (The Nation, 1928); Bartram achieved "the most
distinctive and accomplished style developed by any writer in the
middle colonies" (Literary History of the United States, 1949).

Since the 1950s, new interest in early American literature
has led to increasingly complex analyses of Bartram's artistry. His
language has been examined in its combination of scientific and
poetic dimensions, its classicism, its sense of movement animating
even the inorganic world, its range from the simple to the complex.
Much commentary has focused on his wondrous "painter's eye."
The landscape depicted in Travels has been analyzed for its pictorial
qualities, Bartram's balancing of light and dark, his use of the sub-
lime and the picturesque, and the tension between subjective and objective dimensions in his perception.

III. Images of the Man

William Bartram, says his first biographer (Ord, 1832),
"saw nothing but mildness and harmony in all of nature's works." In
the many retellings of Bartram's life and travels (especially his
journey through the exotic lands of the South) he is usually pre-
sented as a gentle man, highly conscious of beauty and joy in nature,
and the inheritor of a Quaker spirit of sympathy, simplicity and
love. Herbst (1954) proclaims "Everything that he witnesses is ac-
ceptable." Literary critics have taken an interest in the way Bartram reveals himself in his writings, and the narrator of Travels has
been variously characterized and analyzed as romantic hero, self-
effacing persona, adventurous traveler, and spiritual pilgrim.

IV. Artist

Bartram's beautiful and historically important drawings have
occasioned little critical notice, but when they are mentioned they
are usually highly praised. Introducing a collection of drawings
from Bartram's southern trip (1968), Ewan calls Bartram "the one indigenous colonial artist of merit for natural history." Bartram's
achievement in depicting, often for the first time, many species of
American flora and fauna is generally lauded, and his skill as an
artist acknowledged. However, a 1929 essay by Exell of the British
Museum--where many of Bartram's original drawings are housed--con-
tains an accusation which parallels early censure of Bartram's
writing: that he sacrifices realistic proportion to achieve an ar-
tistically balanced picture. Exell backs his claim by reproducing
several Bartram drawings, including an exquisitely surreal scene of
lotuses towering over a wading heron. Perhaps art historians will
reopen the battle over Bartram's relative allegiance to science and
art.

WILLIAM BYRD II (1674-1744)

I. Byrd as Archetype--the Southern Cavalier

"Cavalier" is a word writers in the nineteenth and twentieth
centuries repeatedly use to characterize William Byrd II: cavalier
writer, cavalier planter, inheritor of the cavalier tradition of Old
Virginia. The term implies aristocratic status, an elegant life-
style exhibiting a high level of culture, a character and literary
production marked by charm, wit, detachment, and ubanity. According
to Wright (1940), the Byrd family development illustrates the "progress from trade to genteel elegance" made by important families in
American history. William Byrd I was a merchant prince. William
Byrd II combined the virtues of aristocratic scholar and man of action: he was diligent in public service, built the architecturally
noteworthy Georgian mansion at Westover, and his land-hunger brought
together immense holdings. He bought most of the books in the Byrd

library (one of the finest in colonial America), and read them--
getting up at five or six every morning to read Greek, Latin, Hebrew,
or the modern languages.

Even so distinguished a student of Byrd as Wright describes
Byrd in superlatives: Byrd "lived in greater elegance and with more
fitting grace than any of his contemporaries," and was "the herald
of the eighteenth-century order of Virginia gentlemen." Advocates
of the Old South have seized upon Byrd's reputation and enlarged it
to mythic proportions. For example, in Harland's novel His Great
Self (1892) Byrd is featured as the masterful lord of the plantation
who far outstrips all the other characters in moral strength, learning, culture, intelligence, and wit, and whose one tragic mistake is
his harsh treatment of his daughter Evelyn (a favorite subject of
writers because of the romantic legends of her unhappy love affair,
early death, and return as Westover's resident ghost).

II. The Expansion of Byrd Scholarship

Only one of Byrd's works (A Discourse Concerning the Plague,
with Some Preservations Against It, 1721) was published in his life-
time, and it was issued anonymously. Byrd apparently intended to
publish the History of the Dividing Line, but he chose to continue
the work of polishing with aristocratic disdain for rushing into
print. Consequently, we have no contemporary judgments of Byrd's
work. The first published criticism is by Paulding (1817), who read
the manuscript of the History--"the finest specimen of that . . .
quaint mode of writing fashionable about a century ago, that I have
met with anywhere." Three of Byrd's four travel narratives--The
History of the Dividing Line Betwixt Virginia and North Carolina, A
Journey to the Land of Eden A.D. 1733, and A Progress to the Mines--
were first published as The Westover Manuscripts in 1841 and republished in a more accurate edition in 1866.

The History, frequently described as a classic of American
literature, is generally considered Byrd's best work. The few nine-
teenth-century commentators on Byrd's travel narratives all praise
the History in particular, and laud Byrd's style. The Cyclopaedia
of American Literature (1855) declares Byrd's work sometimes "worthy"
of Fielding, and lauds its vivid descriptions, humor and satire, and
narrative skill. Through the twentieth century, praise for the History continues, and the same qualities are emphasized. Byrd's "zest
for life," his humor and irony, and his acute knowledge of the world;
the "charm" of his prose, its lucidity, and its "racy quality and
idiomatic expression." The History has been characterized as the
"most urbane narrative of the colonial period" (Wright, 1957), and
as the American colonial work which most resembles the style of
Addison and his contemporaries (Marambaud, 1970). Recent analyses
have accorded it a cardinal spot in American literary history: Lynn
(1959) claims Byrd's gentlemanly narrator and elevated style in the
History mark the beginning of Southwestern humor; Davis (1972)

declares that the History becomes "genuine epic . . . a travel-adventure symbolic of the frontier experience."

Bassett's (1901) edition of Byrd's writings included not only the travel narratives but also letters and the first extensive account of Byrd's life. Reviewers praised Byrd's forceful style and quaint humor, and found his work "very candid" (Earle, 1902). In 1904 there appeared the first of a species of Byrd article that counters (or confirms) his criticism of the men of North Carolina. During the first three decades of the twentieth century, the Byrd family was written up a few times, and Parrington and Van Doren stressed the historical importance of the information in Byrd's writings. A series of articles in the Virginia Magazine of History and Biography and William and Mary College Quarterly published some of Byrd's many letters. These letters have drawn attention for literary, as well as biographical and historical, value, with Hubbell (1954) even finding Byrd's letters courting Miss Smith "an epistolary novel in miniature."

The Secret History of the Line (an earlier and more ribald account of the expedition to establish the boundary line between Virginia and North Carolina) was not published until 1929, although it was known in the nineteenth century. Comparisons between the History and Secret History were frequent, beginning with Boyd's 1929 discussion of the differences. The History, however, especially the satirical passages on the lubbers (not in the earlier work) continued to draw most of the attention.

Beatty published William Byrd of Westover, a full-length biography, in 1932. He tried to stress the reality behind the image of the cavalier planter, emphasizing the less glamorous aspects of Byrd's life such as his debts and money problems. But Beatty did not have access to Byrd's secret shorthand diary, discovery of which was announced by Wright in 1939.

Three portions of Byrd's secret diary have been discovered and decoded, covering the periods 1709-1712, 1717-1721, and 1739-1741. These were edited and published over the years 1941-1958 by Wright, Tinling, and Woodfin, who also became major contributors to the critical industry that grew up around the diary. Along with Marambaud and others, they mined this rich vein of information for essays on Byrd's life and times in Augustan London, on the plantation, and in the colonial capital of Williamsburg. Byrd's fascinating revelations recreate the minutiae of his life: frequently fruitless courtships; quarrels and lovemaking with the stormy Lucy Parke and other women; diet; reading; habit of dosing himself and others with home-brewed medicine; amazingly regular habits of work; public service; social life and play; religious practices and beliefs; dreams; superstitions; and relations with friends, enemies, lovers, wives, servants, slaves, and governors.

III. Byrd's Literary Style and Stature

Although a great deal has been published about William Byrd II, and his writings have been constantly praised, most works on Byrd dwell on his activities and the information he provides on his age. Byrd is a man of action who cultivated letters, according to Marambaud (1964), who also states that as a writer Byrd is "essentially an amateur" (1970) and that the diary--the earliest extensive diary by an important Southerner--is disappointing as literature and inferior to Pepys' diary. Marambaud's scholarly biography of Byrd (1971) stresses the importance of the content in Byrd's work, but concludes Byrd lacked "any marked intellectual originality" and that only a small part of his works are "literary."

A few scholars have wrestled with an analysis of Byrd's style. Weathers (1947) elucidates the development of Byrd's epigrammatic style from the early writings which belong to the literary tradition of Augustan London to the later American writings. Lynn, comparing the Secret History with the History, finds a different opposition: the Secret History is written in "a blunt, jerky style, with a tough, unfooled directness that seems unmistakably American," while the History has a "cooly sophisticated" narrator. Schmidt-von Bardeleben (1966) analyzes the grammatical structure and rhythms of the diaries, and declares there is no true break between Byrd's English writings and his later American writings, because the diary already shows the "metaphor free, clear, short style" of the American works. Gummere (1964) discusses Byrd's deceptively casual use of classical allusion; Davis (1972) characterizes the literary texture of Byrd's balanced and paradoxical prose.

Many critics praise Byrd by comparing him to other writers. Byrd is frequently compared to Addison and the other neoclassicists, whose satirical, epigrammatic style was the current ideal; but he is also measured against Fielding, Franklin, Pepys, Boswell, Irving, Crèvecoeur, the Restoration dramatists, and the cavalier poets. Nye (1970) creates a niche for Byrd by declaring his "easy, urbane prose" equal to that of any American writer, except Franklin, before Irving. Franklin is the only colonial writer generally admitted to have surpassed Byrd. Core (1969), however, calls Byrd's prose the "finest" in colonial America. Wright (1957) praises the History as the "most urbane narrative of the colonial period," and Wertenbaker, in the Dictionary of American Biography (1930) agrees that Byrd achieved eminence as a sophisticated writer in a time and place where urbane wit and graceful prose were scarce.

J. HECTOR ST. JOHN DE CRÈVECOEUR (1735-1813)

The qualities for which Crèvecoeur's writings have been valued have undergone near-total transformation in two centuries. Contemporary defenders preferred to identify Crèvecoeur with the uneducated American Farmer who expressed sentimental enthusiasm for his utopian environment. Criticism generally focused on Crèvecoeur's possible inauthenticity. Twentieth-century scholars, by contrast, often praise the same writer for his apparent realism, cynicism, and sophisticated literary technique. The change in image accords with a general transformation of literary values, but new opinions are justified by knowledge of Crèvecoeur manuscripts unpublished until 1925.

I. The Eighteenth Century

During the eighteenth century, Letters from an American Farmer was popular and influential in both English and French editions. Its publication in London, 1782, at first stimulated favorable reviews welcoming the interesting material on America. But 1783 saw Ayscough's slashing attack; Crèvecoeur merely masqueraded as a simple farmer, his glowing picture of America was an insidious enticement to British emigration. Ayscough's pamphlet led to some revised opinions, and opened debate on Crèvecoeur's naïveté and candor.

In Crèvecoeur's native France, each edition--English, 1782; French, 1784; and the expanded French version of 1787--was greeted with favorable reviews. The French audience had an intense interest in America, and, although they were moved by abolitionist sentiments, were pleased to idealize it as a utopian land where the hopes and dreams of mankind were realized.

French reviewers were delighted with Crèvecoeur's untutored style. Lacretelle, one of Crèvecoeur's most enthusiastic promoters, gave Letters very high praise, calling the book "the poetry of America as well as its history." Another reviewer twice called Crèvecoeur "a great poet," sometimes even equal to Homer, for the way he "paints" American scenes. Crèvecoeur's faults were more than compensated for by his primitive poetic talent and his ability to "make the tears run."

German critics were less tolerant than the French of Crèvecoeur's style. A 1782 reviewer did not think the book would interest German readers, who would not have the patience to separate the small amount of gold from the large amount of dross. Nevertheless, two German translations of Letters were published (1784, 1788). The Germans sometimes warned against Crèvecoeur's siren enticements to emigration, but likewise expressed interest in America. They espoused both sides of the debate on the authenticity of the book. Crèvecoeur's ability to stir the heart and his talent for painting America with lively colors were again lauded.

The Netherlands also gave Letters some attention. Reviews of the Dutch translation (1784) show abolitionist sentiment. The Dutch translator and one Dutch reviewer again praised Crèvecoeur's appeal to the feelings.

Introduction

Letters was not reviewed in America as it was in Europe, yet it was popular in the country it describes. According to Mitchell (1916), between the years 1785 and 1805 there were over fifty printings of portions of Letters in periodicals, mostly American serials.

The book's early international reputation cannot be fairly judged from published reviews and critiques. Rice (1933, 1934) proves effectively that Letters was "one of the most read books on America at the end of the eighteenth century." Rice lists the numerous editions and translations: London, 1782; Dublin, 1782; London, 1783; Belfast, 1783; Leipzig, 1784; Leyden, 1784; Paris, 1784, 1785, 1787; Philadelphia, 1793; Leipzig, 1788. He also provides information on the large number of extracts and anecdotes quoted in newspapers, journals, anthologies, and even guide books for immigrants.

II. The Nineteenth Century

Voyage dans la Haute Pensylvanie et dans l'État de New-York was published in 1801. The book was generally well received, and caused attention once more to be focused on Crèvecoeur during 1801-1802. The reviews and the introduction to a German translation commend the book's pictures of the United States and of American Indians.

After the reviews of Voyage, only a few works on Crèvecoeur kept his name alive in the nineteenth century. In France, the first full book on Crèvecoeur was published in 1883--the biography by Robert de Crèvecoeur, Crèvecoeur's great grandson. In America, the Duyckincks (1855) lauded Letters, stressing its idyllic quality, and Tyler (1897) described the book as a "prose pastoral." The only significant treatment of Crèvecoeur by a British writer is also the best in the century: Hazlitt (1829) praised Letters because it conveys "not only the objects, but the feelings of a new country," and has a "liberal, unaffected," at times "homeric" style.

III. The Twentieth Century

Revival: Artless Celebrant of America and Nature

The early twentieth century saw a revival of interest in Crèvecoeur. In 1904, Letters was republished for the first time since the eighteenth century. The introduction by Lewisohn pictures Crèvecoeur as an optimistic celebrant of the American dream. Blake, in an introduction to the English reprint of Letters (1912), called its author an "eighteenth-century Thoreau" whose love of nature gave him modern appeal. A series of later commentators reiterated the same image.

The one dissenting voice--D. H. Lawrence (1919, 1923)-- wrote the most provocative study of Crèvecoeur in the early twentieth century. Lawrence focused on Crèvecoeur as depicter of America and nature, but saw a conflict between Crèvecoeur's pull to primitivism and his insistence on seeing nature as "sweet and pure." Interpretations from 1957 until the present often follow Lawrence in focusing on conflicts in Crèvecoeur's work.

New Material and Approaches

In 1925, Sketches of Eighteenth-Century America was published. It contains eleven of the nineteen sketches Crèvecoeur wrote while living in America before and during the Revolution but did not include in Letters. The publication of these manuscripts was accompanied during 1925-1926 by a barrage of articles from the editors of Sketches (Bourdin, Gabriel, and Williams). The articles discuss the discovery of the manuscripts in France, the nature of the manuscripts, and their importance as sources of information on Crèvecoeur's life and manner of composition. Most important, the articles announce that the traditional view of Crèvecoeur needed modification in two respects: some of the sketches prove that Crèvecoeur was a loyalist rather than a supporter of the American Revolution, and many sketches contain realistic, sometimes harshly realistic observations on America.

Mitchell's 1916 biography attempted to solve puzzles about Crèvecoeur's early life and to provide a detailed account of his work as French consul. Throughout the century, other articles retell Crèvecoeur's long and active life, or focus on specific aspects such as his promotion of scientific projects.

Rice produced the biography of Letters, rather than the biography of its author. Le Cultivateur Américain (1933) is a scholarly study of the stages of development of the book from manuscript through the English and French editions. In addition, Rice provides a detailed study of Crèvecoeur's contemporary reputation and influence on European thought.

In the twentieth century, Voyage has come in for renewed attention and closer scrutiny than it had previously received, owing largely to the efforts of Adams. From 1946 to 1962, Adams studied the book as a valuable source of information on America, examining Crèvecoeur's treatment of the Indian, his sources (especially incorrect attributions and plagiarisms), his style, and the value of the book as literature. Adams concluded that both utopian and realistic elements can be found in Voyage, but he sided with the traditionalists who view Crèvecoeur as essentially a romanticist.

The New Crèvecoeur: Complexity, Disillusion, and Art

The traditional emphasis on Crèvecoeur as optimistic celebrant of America has been promoted in this century not only by Adams but by other critics up to the present. But commentators increasingly have recognized that Crèvecoeur's works show a combination of realism and idyll.

INTRODUCTION

A substantial number of modern critics have departed radically from the idea of Crèvecoeur as sentimental, idealistic, and untrained writer. They have turned the traditional view upside down, spotlighting antithetical qualities: complexity; the tension between the ideal and the real--not merely realism, but also cynicism and disillusionment; the use of sophisticated literary techniques.

Some of these same critics also extol Crèvecoeur's contribution to the American literary tradition. Nye (1969) says the "Yankee" narrator, the tendency to self-analysis, and the vision of America in Letters make it an early landmark in the American tradition. Christadler (1972) declares that Crèvecoeur anticipated later writers who depict the American Adam in the romance. Stone (1962) writes that American literature begins with Letters and its characteristically American techniques, subjects, and themes.

Crèvecoeur's reputation is still changing, and there remain unresolved questions about his writing. Twentieth-century commentators, however, have done much to resurrect the Crèvecoeur who made important contributions to intellectual and social history; and in recent decades, critics have paid close attention to Crèvecoeur's style and his value as a writer, and have effectively demonstrated the importance of his contribution to American literature.

Annotation and Indexing:

Effort was made to include all books and articles in English and foreign languages on the four authors. The preference for fullness of annotation was given to writings from the eighteenth and nineteenth centuries, since these writings are generally more difficult to locate than twentieth-century works. This principle applies especially to the early comments on Crèvecoeur in foreign languages, which constitute an important chapter in the history of his reputation. Occasionally, comments that are significant but very brief are included--Coleridge on William Bartram (1836), for instance.

With the exception of catalogs of the Bartram Garden, all items from John H. Barnhart's "Bartram Bibliography" (1931) have been included. Some of the items listed in Barnhart's bibliography are quite brief, but it seemed best to indicate their true value by annotating them. Articles on the Bartram Garden are included in the section on John Bartram. Books and essays on both Bartrams have been annotated separately whenever the information allowed such division; otherwise, the same annotation is given for both.

Most histories of American literature give a few pages to William Bartram, Byrd, and Crèvecoeur. No effort was made systematically to include all such comments. Anthologies that reprint selections from American authors were excluded.

The annotation is descriptive rather than evaluative. The book is indexed by titles of the works of the four authors, titles of writings about them and their works, authors of these writings, and subjects that are frequently discussed in secondary works on the four authors.

Acknowledgements

I express gratitude to the American Association of University Women for a postdoctoral fellowship for 1974-1975 while I was writing this book; to the University of Texas Research Institute for a special grant for copying and translation; to Frieda Werden for intelligent and resourceful help at all stages of the book; to Rose Bruckbauer Cutting for work on the index; to Edward M. Griffin for help with the introduction; to the staff of the Interlibrary Loan Division at the University of Texas--JoAnne Hawkins, Elaine Albin, Martha Favors, Helen Whitcraft--for patient and generous solicitude in gathering materials.

Abbreviations of List of Works

JOHN BARTRAM

Observations on the Inhabitants, Climate, Soil; Rivers, Productions, Animals, and Other Matters Worthy of Notice. Made by **Mr.** John Bartram, in his Travels from Pensilvania to Onondago, Oswego and the Lake Ontario, in Canada, 1751.   Observations

A Journal, Kept by John Bartram of Philadelphia, Botanist to His Majesty for the Floridas: Upon a Journey from St. Augustine Up the River St. John's, 1767.   Journal

Diary of a Journey through the Carolinas, Georgia, and Florida, 1765-1766, 1944.   Diary

WILLIAM BARTRAM

Travels through North & South Carolina, Georgia, East & West Florida, the Cherokee Country, the Extensive Territories of the Muscogulges, or Creek Confederacy, and the Country of the Chactaws; Containing an Account of the Soil and Natural Productions of those Regions, together with Observations on the Manners of the Indians, 1791.   Travels

WILLIAM BYRD

History of the Dividing Line
Betwixt Virginia and North Caro-
lina, 1841.   History

The Secret History of the
Line, 1929.   Secret History

CRÈVECOEUR

Letters from an American
Farmer; Describing Certain Pro-
vincial Situations, Manners and
Customs, not Generally Known;
and Conveying Some Idea of the
Late and Present Interior Cir-
cumstances of the British
Colonies in North America.
Written for the Information of
a Friend in England, by J.
Hector St. John, a Farmer in
Pennsylvania, 1782.   Letters

Lettres d'un Cultivateur
Américain, Écrites à W. S.
Ecuyer, Depuis l'Année 1770,
jusqu'à 1781. Traduites de
l'Anglois par * * *, 1784,
1787 (in three volumes).   Lettres

Voyage dans la Haute Pen-
sylvanie et dans l'Etat de
New-York, par un Membre Adoptif
de la Nation Onéida. Traduit
et Publié par l'Auteur des
Lettres d'un Cultivateur Améri-
cain, 1801.   Voyage

Sketches of Eighteenth
Century America: More "Letters
from an American Farmer," 1925.   Sketches

List of Periodical Abbreviations

AH	American Heritage
AL	American Literature
AQ	American Quarterly
ArlQ	Arlington Quarterly
EAL	Early American Literature
FHS	French Historical Studies
GaR	Georgia Review
HLQ	Huntington Library Quarterly
HudR	Hudson Review
JEGP	Journal of English and Germanic Philology
MLN	Modern Language Notes
NEQ	New England Quarterly
PAAS	Proceedings of the American Antiquarian Society
PAPS	Proceedings of the American Philosophical Society
PBSA	Papers of the Bibliographical Society of America
PMHB	Pennsylvania Magazine of History and Biography
PMLA	Publications of the Modern Language Association of America
PQ	Philological Quarterly (Iowa City)
SAQ	South Atlantic Quarterly
SatR	Saturday Review
SP	Studies in Philology
SR	Sewanee Review
VC	Virginia Cavalcade
VMHB	Virginia Magazine of History and Biography
VQR	Virginia Quarterly Review
WMQ	William and Mary Quarterly
YR	Yale Review
YSE	Yale Studies in English

Writings About John Bartram, 1751 - 1974

1751 A   BOOKS - NONE

1751 B   SHORTER WRITINGS

1   [JACKSON.] "Preface," in Observations on the Inhabitants, Climate, Soil, Rivers, Productions, Animals, and Other Matters Worthy of Notice. Made by Mr. John Bartram, in His Travels from Pensilvania to Onondago, Oswego and the Lake Ontario, in Canada. To Which is Annex'd, a Curious Account of the Cataracts at Niagara. By Mr. Peter Kalm a Swedish Gentleman Who Travelled There. London: J. Whiston and B. White, pp. i-viii.

      Laments the fact Bartram did not have a "literal education," hence his "stile" is "not so clear as we could wish." However, his writing shows "marks of much good sense, penetration, and sincerity, join'd to a commendable curiosity." The journal was made public without the author's knowledge; if intended for publication, he probably would have made it more entertaining and abridged it. "This plain yet sensible piece merits attention" because of the importance of the area described to the future of Great Britain.

1767 A   BOOKS - NONE

1767 B   SHORTER WRITINGS

1   ANON. "An Extract of Mr. Wm. [sic] Bartram's Observations in a Journey up the River Savannah in Georgia with His Son, on Discoveries," Gentleman's Magazine, XXXVII (April), 166-68.

      Introduces an extract from John Bartram's journal of his Florida trip, 1765-1766. The British commentator notes that Bartram was "very superficial in his descriptions of places, but has mentioned many plants and soils, which, to the people of this island, do not seem of much consequence."

1767

2   STORK, WILLIAM. "The Introduction," in An Account of East-
         Florida, with a Journal, Kept by John Bartram of Philadel-
         phia, Botanist to His Majesty for the Floridas; upon a
         Journey from St. Augustine up the River St. John's.
         London: W. Nicoll, pp. iii-viii.
            Publishes John Bartram's journal to supply information on
         the soil and climate of East-Florida and to compare the
         advantages and disadvantages of settling there. John Bar-
         tram is "well known, and well respected in the learned
         world, as an able Naturalist." The usefulness of the
         journal shows the usefulness of his appointment as botanist
         to his Majesty.

1770 A BOOKS - NONE

1770 B SHORTER WRITINGS

1   KALM, PETER. Travels into North America. Translated by John
         Forster. London: The editor. Reprint. Barre, Mass.:
         The Imprint Society, 1972, pp. 65-78.
            John Bartram was "born with a peculiar genius for sci-
         ences." He has traveled extensively and discovered many
         hitherto unknown plants. He "lets nothing escape notice,"
         but deserves blame for not writing down all his observa-
         tions. Hence the published account of his travels has
         "few new observations." "He has not filled it with a
         thousandth part of the great knowledge he has acquired."
         Kalm admits that he is indebted to Bartram for "many things"
         and frequently cites Bartram as the source of his informa-
         tion.

1782 A BOOKS - NONE

1782 B SHORTER WRITINGS

1   CRÈVECOEUR, MICHEL GUILLAUME JEAN DE. "Letter XI. From Mr.
         Iw-n Al-z, a Russian Gentleman; Describing the Visit He
         Paid at My Request to Mr. John Bartram, the Celebrated
         Pennsylvanian Botanist," in Letters from an American Farmer.
         London: T. Davies and Davis, pp. 247-69.
            A visit to John Bartram recounted by a (probably ficti-
         tious) Russian traveler. Extols the Quaker simplicity of
         Bartram's life. He has freed his slaves and treats them
         as members of his family. Bartram, a model farmer, dis-
         cusses his methods of farming. While ploughing, Bartram's
         curiosity was awakened by a daisy; this incident inspired

2

(CRÈVECOEUR, MICHEL GUILLAUME JEAN DE)
him to study botany. His studies gave him a "general
knowledge of every plant and tree" on the continent.
Praises Bartram as "the first man whose name as a botanist
hath done honour to America."

1804 A BOOKS - NONE

1804 B SHORTER WRITINGS

1   BARTRAM, WILLIAM. "Some Account of the Late Mr. John Bartram,
         of Pennsylvania," Philadelphia Medical and Physical Journal,
         I (13 November), 115-24.
            Tells the history of the Bartrams in America before John
         Bartram. John Bartram had little formal education and
         first studied nature from behind the plough. An interest
         in physic and surgery probably led him to botany. He was
         perhaps the first Anglo-American to establish a botanic
         garden. Largely through the help of Collinson, Bartram be-
         came a correspondent of European notables. Discusses the
         areas of the United States he traveled through, giving most
         attention to his trip to Florida. Extols his virtues and
         describes his physical appearance. He was educated a
         Quaker, but his religious creed was independent of sects.

1827 A BOOKS - NONE

1827 B SHORTER WRITINGS

1   ANON. "Florida," American Quarterly Review, II (September),
         226.
            Bartram's book on Florida (1767) "appears to be out of
         print at present, although it is well worthy of preserva-
         tion, among a collection devoted to the illustration of the
         natural history of Florida."

1831 A BOOKS - NONE

1831 B SHORTER WRITINGS

1   MEASE, JAMES. "Bartram's Botanic Garden on the Schuylkill,
         near Philadelphia," Gardener's Magazine and Register of
         Rural and Domestic Improvement, VII (December), 665-66.
            Bartram's Garden was "the first attempt to establish a
         garden for the reception and cultivation of native and

1832

(MEASE, JAMES)
foreign plants and trees in North America." Sketches John
Bartram's biography (study of botany, travels, correspondence, exportation of plants and seeds, honors). He was the
first to regularly export American plants to Europe. See
also (WB1831.B1).

1832 A BOOKS - NONE

1832 B SHORTER WRITINGS

1   M.[EASE], J.[AMES]. "Foreign Notices: North America. Bartram's
       Botanic Garden on the Schuylkill, near Philadelphia,"
       Gardener's Magazine and Register of Rural and Domestic Im-
       provements, VII, 665-66.
           Bartram is the "first naturalist the United States had,
       and the first American scientific horticulturist." The
       garden is about ten miles southwest of Philadelphia. "The
       present proprietor, Mr. Robert Carr, who married the daugh-
       ter of John, enlarged the garden, and has been extensively
       engaged in the business of it for several years past."

2   [ORD, GEORGE.] "Biographical Sketch of William Bartram,"
       Cabinet of Natural History and Rural Sports, with Illus-
       trations, II, i-vii.
           Biographical sketch of John Bartram, "a celebrated and
       self-taught philosopher and botanist." Bartram pursued
       knowledge so earnestly he usually read while eating his
       meals. He was the "first American who conceived and exe-
       cuted the design of a botanic garden." His advances in
       learning, botany and other sciences led to his correspond-
       ence with many noted men and his work in collecting plants
       for European gardens.
       Reprinted as American Philosophical Society Pamphlet V.
       (1832.B3); see also (WB1832.B1).

3   _____. "Biographical Sketch of William Bartram with Por-
       trait," American Philosophical Society Pamphlet V, 1166.
           Reprinted from Cabinet of Natural History and Rural
       Sports (JB1832.B2).

4   WYNNE, WILLIAM. "Some Account of the Nursery Gardens and the
       State of Horticulture in the Neighborhood of Philadelphia,
       with Remarks on the Subject of the Emigration of British
       Gardeners to the United States," Gardener's Magazine and
       Register of Rural and Domestic Improvement, VIII (June),
       272-77.

(WYNNE, WILLIAM)
    Bartram's Botanic Garden deserves first mention among
Philadelphia gardens because of age (100 years) and "from
its containing the best collection of American plants in
the United States." Names specific species from among the
2000 represented. The nursery has "large specimens of all
the rare American trees and shrubs."

1849 A BOOKS - NONE

1849 B SHORTER WRITINGS

1   DARLINGTON, WILLIAM. "Advertisement," in Memorials of John
        Bartram and Humphry Marshall, edited by William Darlington.
        Philadelphia: Lindsay and Blakison, pp. iii-v.
            Darlington was given permission to edit and publish the
        correspondence of Humphry Marshall and John Bartram by
        descendants of the two men. Much of John Bartram's corres-
        pondence is "irrecoverably lost." The manuscripts were
        "generally much injured by time, and many of them scarcely
        legible." Bartram was "the Botanical Patriarch of our
        country." The most reliable biographical account is prob-
        ably the one written by his son William (JB1804.B1).

2   _____. "Biographical Sketch of John Bartram," in Memorials of
        John Bartram and Humphry Marshall, edited by William Dar-
        lington. Philadelphia: Lindsay and Blakison, pp. 37-57.
            John Bartram was "the earliest native American Botanist,
        and the founder of the first Botanical Garden on this con-
        tinent." Quotes William Bartram's account of his father
        (JB1804.B1) and Crèvecoeur's description of Bartram in
        Letters from an American Farmer (JB1782.B1). Supplies ad-
        ditional information on Bartram's genealogy, descendants,
        marriages, and death.

3   _____. "Progress of Botany in North America," in Memorials of
        John Bartram and Humphry Marshall, edited by William Dar-
        lington. Philadelphia: Lindsay and Blakison, pp. 2-33.
            John Bartram was "passionately fond" of natural history
        from youth. "He probably detected more undescribed plants
        than any of his contemporaries in our country." He was
        also probably the first to start a botanic garden in
        British America. Bartram was aided greatly by Collinson,
        who constantly encouraged him to study American plants and
        to collect and send them to England. Bartram carried on
        this work "with indefatigable labour through a long course
        of years, and with amazing success." Bartram conducted a
        series of experiments on sex in plants.

1850

<u>1850 A BOOKS - NONE</u>

<u>1850 B SHORTER WRITINGS</u>

1   ANON. "Trees and Pleasure Grounds in Pennsylvania," <u>Horti-</u>
           <u>culturist</u>, V (December), 251-55.
              Includes an account of a visit to Bartram's Garden.
           Andrew M. Eastwick, the present owner, intends to preserve
           the garden as a monument to John Bartram. Because of Bar-
           tram's wide travels, the garden probably contains more in-
           digenous trees than any other place of the same size. Dis-
           cusses the history of individual trees. Describes some of
           the trees, plants, and buildings in the garden. Washington,
           Jefferson, and Franklin visited Bartram's Garden.
           Reprinted in a revised form as "Account of the Bartram
           Garden" (JB1864.B1; JB1929.B1).

<u>1851 A BOOKS - NONE</u>

<u>1851 B SHORTER WRITINGS</u>

1   DILLINGHAM, WILLIAM HENRY. "Peter Collinson," <u>The Biblical</u>
           <u>Repertory</u> and <u>Princeton</u> <u>Review</u>, XXIII (July), 416-450.
              Collinson did more than anyone else to help John Bartram.
           Bartram and Humphry Marshall were self-educated farmers who
           approached nature with wonder. "No two men in this country
           ever contributed so much to the botanical treasures of
           England..." Quotes an "effusion" on the colors and shapes
           of flowers to prove John Bartram's "genius." Quotes ex-
           tensively from the Collinson/Bartram correspondence, de-
           voting most space to Bartram's hostility to the Indians.
           Bartram's Garden "has been an object of interest the world
           over for a century past."
           Reprinted as <u>A</u> <u>Tribute</u> <u>to</u> <u>the</u> <u>Memory</u> <u>of</u> <u>Peter</u> <u>Collinson</u>
           <u>with</u> <u>Some</u> <u>Notice</u> <u>of</u> <u>Dr.</u> <u>Darlington's</u> <u>Memorials</u> <u>of</u> <u>John</u>
           <u>Bartram</u> <u>and</u> <u>Humphry</u> <u>Marshall</u>. (JB1852.B1).

<u>1852 A BOOKS - NONE</u>

<u>1852 B SHORTER WRITINGS</u>

1   DILLINGHAM, WILLIAM HENRY. <u>A</u> <u>Tribute</u> <u>to</u> <u>the</u> <u>Memory</u> <u>of</u> <u>Peter</u>
           <u>Collinson</u> <u>with</u> <u>Some</u> <u>Notice</u> <u>of</u> <u>Dr.</u> <u>Darlington's</u> <u>Memorials</u>
           <u>of</u> <u>John</u> <u>Bartram</u> <u>and</u> <u>Humphry</u> <u>Marshall</u>. Philadelphia: Henry
           Longstreth.
              Reprinted from "Peter Collinson," <u>Biblical</u> <u>Repertory</u> <u>and</u>
           <u>Princeton</u> <u>Review</u> (JB1851.B1).

1859 A   BOOKS – NONE

1859 B   SHORTER WRITINGS

1   ALLIBONE, SAMUEL A.   "Bartram, John," in A Critical Dictionary
        of English Literature and British and American Authors.
        Vol. I.   Philadelphia: J. B. Lippencott Company.   Re-
        printed Detroit: Gale Research Co., 1965, 137.
            Bartram was "an eminent botanist" who "took great pleas-
        ure" in his botanical garden.   Quotes Linnaeus's praise of
        Bartram as the "greatest natural" botanist in the world.
        Lists names of men who encouraged and helped him.   Gives
        the titles of his published journals.

2   SIMPSON, HENRY.   "John Bartram," in The Lives of Eminent
        Philadelphians, Now Deceased.   Philadelphia: W. Brother-
        head, pp. 31-36.
            Gives the description of John Bartram from Letters from
        an American Farmer.   Bartram's first passion for the study
        of botany was "excited by his contemplating a simple daisy."
        He achieved early success in the study of medicine and sur-
        gery.   Since most medicine came from the vegetable kingdom,
        he probably learned to value botany in this way.   Discusses
        Bartram's travels to collect specimens of plants and fos-
        sils.

1860 A   BOOKS – NONE

1860 B   SHORTER WRITINGS

1   ANON.   "The Bartram Tribute: Published as an Auxiliary Aid
        to the Purposes of the Festival Given by the Ladies of St.
        James' Episcopal Church, 'Bartram Garden,' Kingsessing,
        June 13 & 14, 1860."
            Biographical sketch of John Bartram, quoting in entirety
        William Bartram's account of his father (JB1804.B1), adding
        details on Bartram's marriages and death.   Also reprints in
        entirety Crèvecoeur's account of Bartram (JB1782.B1).
        Includes a brief article on Bartram and the Indians, de-
        claring that he was never menaced by them during his
        travels and quoting a 1751 poem that pictures Bartram as
        protected from all danger by "Innocence" rather than wea-
        pons.   Also prints a nineteenth-century poem in praise of
        the house and Bartram's Garden.

2   L[IPPINCOTT, JAMES S.]   "Sketches of Philadelphia Botanists:
        John and William Bartram and Humphrey Marshall," Gardener's
        Monthly and Horticulturist, II (September), 271-73.

1862

(LIPPINCOTT, JAMES S.)
John Bartram was a self-educated farmer. According to a story, the governor of Pennsylvania mistook Bartram for a simple farmer until the latter amazed him by speaking in a series of learned languages. Bartram was "not only a man of science, a man of genius and a man of great capacities--he was a man of great virtues." The Bartram Garden is well worth visiting. Discusses plants in the garden in 1860. <u>See also</u> (WB1860.B1).

1862 A BOOKS - NONE

1862 B SHORTER WRITINGS

1   SMITH, GEORGE. "Bartram, John," in <u>History of Delaware County, Pennsylvania</u>. Philadelphia: Henry B. Ashmead, pp. 444-45.
       Factual biographical sketch of John Bartram, "the earliest of American botanists, and the first to establish a botanic garden in America." This "great man" educated himself and turned to the study of nature while working in the field. Discusses his marriages, religion, death.

1864 A BOOKS - NONE

1864 B SHORTER WRITINGS

1   ANON. "Account of the Bartram Garden." Philadelphia: C. Sherman, Son & Co.
       Reprinted with revisions from <u>Horticulturist</u> (JB1850.B1). Reissued with additional material (JB1929.B1).

2   TUCKERMAN, HENRY T. <u>America and Her Commentators: With a Critical Sketch of Travel in the United States</u>. New York: Charles Scribner, pp. 372-82.
       Summarizes John Bartram's life and work. <u>Observations</u> "retains the charm of ingenuous zeal, integrity, and kindliness." Follows Bartram's itinerary and notes some observations on natural objects, the landscape, Indian life, white settlements. With "honest zeal and intelligent observation ... [he] recorded the wonders and beauty of the scene" when he traveled to Florida at an advanced age. At home on his farm, Bartram embodied "the idea of a rural citizen of America."

1871 A BOOKS - NONE

1871 B SHORTER WRITINGS

1   PARTON, JAMES. "John Bartram: The Self-taught American
        Botanist," Wood's Household Magazine [Illustrated Household
        Magazine], IX (October), 167-69.
            Eulogistic biography. Bartram "never had an enemy and
        his whole life was goodness and benevolence." Bartram
        turned to botany after examining a daisy. "There is
        scarcely any American plant, suited to the soil and climate
        of England, which is not cultivated there," thanks to the
        efforts of John Bartram.

1880 A BOOKS - NONE

1880 B SHORTER WRITINGS

1   PYLE, HOWARD. "Bartram and His Garden," Harper's New Monthly
        Magazine, LX (February), 321-30.
            Describes the house where John Bartram lived, the grounds
        and garden (present condition and changes since Bartram's
        time). Quotes passages from Crèvecoeur's account of John
        Bartram as undoubtedly presenting a true description of his
        simple, admirable life. John Bartram's own letters give
        readers "the life, the manners, the customs, of the time
        in which he lived."

1885 A BOOKS - NONE

1885 B SHORTER WRITINGS

1   MEEHAN, THOMAS. "The Old Botanic Garden of Bartram," Gar-
        dener's Monthly and Horticulturist, XXVII (January), 26-27.
            Descendants of John Bartram propose a Bartram "family
        organization," which might purchase Bartram's homestead and
        garden. The garden was in danger of destruction, but an
        ordinance gives the city the right to take land for public
        squares.

1889

1889 A BOOKS - NONE

1889 B SHORTER WRITINGS

1   [SARGENT, CHARLES S.] Garden and Forest, II (20 February),
       86.
              Letters from Philadelphia indicate there is an oppor-
       tunity to acquire Bartram's Garden for public use. Calls
       for funds from public-spirited citizens to aid this project.
       "This spot has for years been the Mecca of botanists and
       horticulturists."

2   _____. Garden and Forest, II (6 March), 120.
              The Common Council of Philadelphia has authorized the
       city to negotiate for purchase of Bartram's Garden to serve
       as a public park. Some stable corporation like the Academy
       of Natural Science or the University of Pennsylvania should
       manage the new park.

3   _____. Garden and Forest, II (27 March), 156.
              The Philadelphia Select Council passed an ordinance
       appropriating Bartram's Garden for park purposes.

1891 A BOOKS - NONE

1891 B SHORTER WRITINGS

1   ANON. "The Bartram Library," Philadelphia Public Ledger
       (11 September), p. 6.
              The remains of John Bartram's library, books belonging to
       William Bartram and other members of the Bartram family,
       and various family relics have been donated to the His-
       torical Society of Pennsylvania. The collection (which
       includes many rare books) totals about 100 volumes. Lists
       specific books (among them, William Bartram's own copy of
       Travels).

2   [MEEHAN, THOMAS.] "John Bartram," Meehan's Monthly, I
       (August), 31.
              Councilman Meehan has succeeded in preserving Bartram's
       Garden as a public park. It was planted in 1720 when John
       Bartram was 19; many of the trees are in a fair state of
       preservation.

1892 A BOOKS - NONE

1892 B SHORTER WRITINGS

1   [YOUMANS, WILLIAM J.] "Sketch of John and William Bartram,"
         Popular Science Monthly, XL (April), 827-39.
              John and William Bartram were among "the earliest and
         most notable" students of American natural history. De-
         tailed account of John Bartram's life, largely using the
         information provided by William Darlington and John Bar-
         tram's letters, especially those to Collinson. Discusses
         John Bartram's correspondence with other scientists and
         collectors, his journeys and journals. The journal de-
         scribing Florida proves he "was not a ready writer," al-
         though "his observations are minute and sagacious." Sum-
         marizes the later history of Bartram's Garden, which became
         a city park in 1891. See also (WB1892.B2).

1893 A BOOKS - NONE

1893 B SHORTER WRITINGS

1   ANON. "At Bartram's Garden: Read at a Reunion of the Descend-
         ants of John Bartram, Held at the Garden, Sixth Month, 8th,
         1893."
              A poem celebrating John Bartram's "complete/ And beauti-
         ful" life and his work as botanist and gardener. "Kind
         mother Nature" showed John Bartram "her secret treasures."
         His garden is still the resort of the "successive genera-
         tions," and its fame has spread "far across the world."

2   [MEEHAN, THOMAS.] "John Bartram," Meehan's Monthly, III
         (August), 126.
              Bartram was interested in "every good work that had re-
         lation to humanity." He contributed to the first subscrip-
         tion library in Pennsylvania (1743) and secured Collinson's
         aid for the library.

3   WHITCOMB, SELDEN L. "Nature in Early American Literature,"
         SR, II (November), 159-79.
              Discusses John Bartram among other early American
         writers. Bartram deserves attention for his historical
         importance and attractive qualities as man and botanist.
         His correspondence is generally "dull reading," but has
         passages "remarkable for sly mother-wit or unconscious
         humor." He wrote usually as "a mere chronicler of nature"
         but sometimes expressed his love of nature in "highly
         rhetorical passages."

1895

<u>1895 A BOOKS - NONE</u>

<u>1895 B SHORTER WRITINGS</u>

1   BUNTING, MORGAN. "Genealogical Chart of the Bunting Family."
            Darby, Pa.: [Broadside].
               Sarah Bunting married James Bartram (the son of John, the
            botanist) in 1752. Descendants include Samuel, James, and
            Ann Bartram. No other Bartrams are represented. Incor-
            rectly listed in Barnhart's bibliography (JB1931.B1) as
            "Genealogical Chart of the Bartram Family."

<u>1896 A BOOKS - NONE</u>

<u>1896 B SHORTER WRITINGS</u>

1   DOCK, MIRA L. "Bartram's Garden Today," <u>Garden</u> <u>and</u> <u>Forest</u>,
            IX (25 March), 122-24.
               The approach of the 200th anniversary of John Bartram's
            birth in 1699 should stir interest in the work being done
            on his garden (now owned by the city of Philadelphia).
            The University of Pennsylvania is restoring the house and
            grounds to original conditions. Describes the layout of
            the grounds and locates specific plants. Describes the
            house and reproduces two photographs of it.

2   [MEEHAN, THOMAS.] "John Bartram's Wood-Shed," <u>Meehan's</u>
            <u>Monthly</u>, VI (January), 11, 17.
               Reproduces a photograph of John Bartram's wood-shed,
            which functioned as his potting and packing shed. "Doubt-
            less most of the cherished plants of Collinson and other
            English worthies saw the light of America for the last
            time here."

3   [SARGENT, CHARLES S.] "John Bartram," <u>Garden</u> <u>and</u> <u>Forest</u>, IX
            (25 March), 121.
               Applauds the preservation of John Bartram's garden, the
            first memorial of this type given to an American naturalist.
            Bartram's "love of plants showed him his field for doing
            good in the world, and made him a traveler and discoverer
            at a time when no other American was interested in botany."
            By modern standards, his garden is a humble one, but in his
            time the plants were unknown and had to be gathered with
            great difficulty.

4   YOUMANS, WILLIAM J. "John Bartram, 1699-1777, and William
            Bartram, 1739-1823," in <u>Pioneers</u> <u>of</u> <u>Science</u> <u>in</u> <u>America</u>.

(YOUMANS, WILLIAM J.)
New York: D. Appleton and Co. Reprinted. Ann Arbor, Mich.: University Microfilms, 1965, pp. 24-39.
John Bartram's life, stressing his contribution to science. Crèvecoeur's account "in all important respects... represents the botanist as he was." Quotes liberally from Bartram's correspondence with Collinson and others. The journal of his Florida trip is "the barest statement of facts," but the observations are "minute and sagacious." Bartram experimented with the sexual parts of plants and cross fertilization, was interested in geology, was not much of a zoologist. See also (WB1896.B1).

1897 A   BOOKS - NONE

1897 B   SHORTER WRITINGS

1   ANON. "Bartram, John," in The National Cyclopaedia of American Biography, Being the History of the United States. Vol. VII. New York: J. T. White and Company. Reprinted. Ann Arbor, Mich.: University Microfilms, 1967, 153-54.
         Stresses John Bartram's lack of advantages. "Self taught ... he surmounted all obstacles." Discusses his studies, work as a farmer and builder, travels, friends, correspondence. Quotes praise by Linnaeus and Logan. Bartram sent many plants to "enrich European gardens." He was famous abroad, "ever a consistent Christian," and "a consistent opponent of slavery."

2   BAILEY, LIBERTY H. "In Bartram's Garden," Meehan's Monthly, VII (March), 50.
         Includes a poem by Bailey, "In Bartram's Garden": Bartram's "simple spirit" lives on in his garden. In 1870 Bartram's Garden was in danger of being sold for building purposes. Meehan accepted a city council seat and succeeded in saving the park. The city added 18 more acres of Bartram's farm to enlarge the Bartram Park.

1899 A   BOOKS - NONE

1899 B   SHORTER WRITINGS

1   HARSHBERGER, JOHN W. "John Bartram," in The Botanists of Philadelphia and Their Work. Philadelphia: T. C. Davis, pp. 46-76.

1900

(HARSHBERGER, JOHN W.)
Surveys John Bartram's botanical correspondence and describes the shipments to Collinson. Gives an account of
Bartram's travels. Provides a detailed survey of the Bartram house as it appeared in 1899. Describes the grounds
and the garden in detail. Quotes from an 1830 report on
the number and types of plants grown in the garden. Gives
the history of efforts to reclaim and preserve the garden.

2   [MEEHAN, THOMAS.] "History of John Bartram," Meehan's Monthly,
IX (June), 96.
The Bartram legend presents John Bartram as an "ignoramus"
moved by the beauty of a daisy to study nature. His son
William Bartram gave the true account, declaring that John
Bartram loved natural history from youth and took a course
in medicine before deciding to devote himself to botany.
He was not the ignorant man some biographers describe.

1900 A BOOKS - NONE

1900 B SHORTER WRITINGS

1   MILLER, WILLIAM T. "Bartram, John," in Cyclopedia of American
Horticulture, edited by Liberty H. Bailey. Vol. I. New
York: Macmillan Co., 133.
Sketch of Bartram's life and labors. "Bartram was probably the first American to perform successful experiments
in hybridization." A genus of mosses and an oak bear his
name. The services of the garden were very great. Praises
Bartram's study of aboriginal races, and his "simple,
wholesome, powerful personality." Calls for new editions
of Bartram's works.
Reprinted, with slight modifications, in Standard Cyclopedia of Horticulture (JB1914.B2).

1902 A BOOKS - NONE

1902 B SHORTER WRITINGS

1   [NITZSCHE, GEORGE E.] "The Bartram Memorial Library," Old
Pennsylvania Weekly Review, I (5 December), 1.
The Bartram Memorial Library at the University of Pennsylvania was begun by the Bartram Association. Efforts
are being made to make it a good collection of American
botanical books, including books from 1750 to 1850. Lists
specific additions to the library.

1904 A BOOKS - NONE

1904 B SHORTER WRITINGS

1   [ABBOTT, ELIZABETH O.] "Bartram's Garden, Philadelphia, Pa."
        Philadelphia: The John Bartram Association.
            Biography of John Bartram. Bartram was able "to make a
        garden in a wilderness; to make the wilderness tributary
        to it; and it tributary to the great centres of learning
        and thought on another continent." Bartram extended human
        knowledge through his difficult and perilous journeys, his
        botanical correspondence (with "all the distinguished
        naturalists of his time"), and his work in supplying seeds
        to British patrons.
        Reissued in an expanded version (JB1907.B1; JB1915.B1).

2   LOVELL, JOHN H. "The Beginnings of American Science: The
        First Botanist," New England Magazine, n.s. XXX (August),
        753-67.
            The demand for American plants by English gardeners and
        horticulturists stimulated the study of botany during the
        eighteenth century. John Bartram was encouraged by Col-
        linson and other English patrons to collect and study
        American plants. The Bartram/Collinson correspondence
        provides "an extremely interesting picture of the condition
        of botany and horticulture in the times of the colonies."
        Describes Bartram's travels and summarizes the work of
        other early American botanists that Bartram knew.

1905 A BOOKS - NONE

1905 B SHORTER WRITINGS

1   CAPEN, BRONSON C. "Chapter XVII: John Bartram," in Country
        Homes of Famous Americans. New York: Doubleday, Page &
        Co., pp. 157-61.
            Introduces John Bartram's work as a botanist. Describes
        the stone farmhouse that Bartram built; both inside and
        outside are "quaint and unconventional." Photographs show
        modern views of the house and grounds; an old print shows
        how it looked in the past.

1906

1906 A   BOOKS - NONE

1906 B   SHORTER WRITINGS

1   BRITTEN, JAMES. "Bibliographical Notes. XXXVIII. John
        Bartram's Travels," Journal of Botany, British and Foreign,
        XLIV (June), 213, 214.
           Lists biographical data, selected primary and secondary
        sources.

2   JACKSON, M. KATHERINE. "Outlines of the Literary History of
        Colonial Pennsylvania," Columbia University Studies in
        English and Comparative Literature, XIII, 104-5.
           Brief summary of John Bartram's life and work. His Ob-
        servations lacks the literary quality of his son's work,
        yet it shows that John Bartram was "keen and discriminating."

1907 A   BOOKS - NONE

1907 B   SHORTER WRITINGS

1   ABBOTT, ELIZABETH O. "Bartram's Garden, Philadelphia, Pa."
        Philadelphia: The John Bartram Association.
           An expanded version of the JB1904.B1 issue of this essay.
        It includes a plan of the garden in 1907, a lengthy de-
        scription of significant plants and trees, a description
        of the cider mill and procedures to be followed in re-
        storing it, and a description of John Bartram's house.
        Reprinted (JB1915.B1).

1912 A   BOOKS - NONE

1912 B   SHORTER WRITINGS

1   W[ATERSON], D[AVINIA]. "Bartram, John (1699-1778)," in A
        Cyclopedia of American Medical Biography, edited by Howard
        A. Kelly. Vol. I. Philadelphia: Saunders Co., 56-57.
           Tells the story of Bartram's conversion to botany through
        an encounter with a daisy. He prepared the notes and ap-
        pendix to Short's Medicina Britannica (1751). Gives a
        short account of his journeys and correspondence. Bartram
        treated his slaves humanely and anticipated Tolstoy's
        "simple life."
        Reprinted with revisions in American Medical Biographies
        (JB1920.B2).

1913 A BOOKS - NONE

1913 B SHORTER WRITINGS

1   [STICKLEY, GUSTAV.] "A Picturesque Old House in Philadelphia
        Recalling the Adventurous Lives of John and William Bar-
        tram, Early American Botanists," The Craftsman, XXIV (May),
        193-97.
            Brief description of the Bartram house in Philadelphia
        (built in 1731). See also (WB1913.B1).

1914 A BOOKS - NONE

1914 B SHORTER WRITINGS

1   KELLY, HOWARD A. "John Bartram," in Some American Medical
        Botanists. Troy, N. Y.: Southworth Company, pp. 49-59.
            John Bartram was America's earliest botanist and the
        founder of America's first botanical garden. He had an
        early inclination to medicine. Summarizes his life. He
        was "a genial philanthropist" who anticipated Tolstoy in
        "the simple life." Quotes from Collinson's and Baldwin's
        letters to Bartram. Dr. Gordon wrote disparagingly of
        his abilities. Several plants were named after him.

2   MILLER, WILLIAM T. "Bartram, John," in Standard Cyclopedia
        of Horticulture, edited by Liberty H. Bailey. Vol. I.
        New York: Macmillan Co., pp. 1564-65.
            Reprinted, with slight modifications, from Cyclopedia of
        American Horticulture (JB1900.B1).

1915 A BOOKS - NONE

1915 B SHORTER WRITINGS

1   ABBOTT, ELIZABETH O. "Bartram's Garden. Philadelphia, Pa."
        Philadelphia: The John Bartram Association.
        Reissued from (JB1907.B1).

2   *ANON. "Bartram Garden. Specimens of Nearly Every Plant in
        Eastern North America Have Disappeared from Garden John
        Bartram made Famous. Movement Started to Restore Workyard
        of Former Prominent Botanist," Public Ledger, Philadelphia
        (28 June).
            Unlocatable. National Union Catalog, Pre-1956 Imprints,
        p. 104.

17

1917

3   FOX, RICHARD HINGSTON. "John Bartram, Botanist," Friends'
         Quarterly Examiner, no. 194 (April), pp. 145-53.
           Biographical account. "John Bartram was a Quaker, as
      were his forebears, and it was the Friendly habit of
      thought, the simplicity of mind, the readiness to contem-
      plate, the sense of being ever in the Presence, that gave
      to Bartram much of his charm as a botanist." Discusses
      Bartram's family background, study of botany, the garden
      ("a model of scientific culture, as well as the home of
      rare vegetable forms"), friends and patrons, exportation
      of seeds, travels.

1917 A BOOKS - NONE

1917 B SHORTER WRITINGS

1   BARNHART, JOHN H. Journal of the New York Botanical Garden
         Bulletin, XVIII (November), n. 239.
           Footnote on John Bartram's life, "the first native Ameri-
      can botanist." He was greatly encouraged by Collinson.
      He traveled and collected from New York to Florida.

2   CLARK, BERTHA. "Bartram's Garden," The House Beautiful, XLI
         (March), 205-207, 262-63, 266.
           History of Bartram's Garden. Incorporates quotations
      from his correspondence into a character sketch of John
      Bartram. Photographs illustrate that "the old stone house
      is standing, and some of the fine trees Bartram planted
      are living, but many of the most beautiful specimens are
      dead."

3   COOPER, LANE. "Travellers and Observers, 1763-1846," in The
         Cambridge History of American Literature, edited by William
      P. Trent, et al. Vol. I. New York: G. P. Putnam's Sons.
      Reprinted. New York: Macmillan Co., 1946, pp. 194-95.
         Brief description of John Bartram's life and work
      (travels, reputation as a botanist, botanic garden,
      European correspondence).

1919 A BOOKS - NONE

1919 B SHORTER WRITINGS

1   FOX, RICHARD HINGSTON. Dr. John Fothergill and His Friends:
         Chapters in Eighteenth Century Life. London: Macmillan
      and Co., pp. 159-71.

1921

(FOX, RICHARD HINGSTON)
"Bartram was a born naturalist; his eye seemed never to miss a fresh object, and nothing escaped his memory." Describes the range of Bartram's travels. He was hostile to Indians, who hindered his travels. Discusses the problems of sending specimens to England. Collinson and Bartram speculated on natural history. Bartram was disowned by the Friends for Unitarian beliefs. Sketches the history of Bartram's Garden after his death.

1920 A BOOKS - NONE

1920 B SHORTER WRITINGS

1   HARSHBERGER, JOHN W. "The Old Gardens of Pennsylvania: I.--
         Bartram Arboretum and Park," The Garden Magazine, XXXII
         (October), 78-80.
              Brief introduction to John Bartram's life and botanical
         work. The arboretum was begun in 1730. Describes the
         history and present condition of specific trees. Reprints
         photographs of the house and some of the trees.

2   [WATERSON, DAVINIA.] "Bartram, John," in American Medical
         Biographies, edited by Howard A. Kelly, and Walter L.
         Burrage. Baltimore: Norman Remington, pp. 70-71.
              Reprints with slight modifications the article from A
         Cyclopedia of American Medical Biography (JB1912.B1).

1921 A BOOKS - NONE

1921 B SHORTER WRITINGS

1   BARNHART, JOHN H. Journal of the New York Botanical Garden,
         XXII (July), n. 127.
              A footnote on John Bartram's life. He was self-taught
         of necessity. He established the first botanic garden in
         America. For nearly 50 years, "an almost continuous stream
         of American seeds and plants, sent by Bartram, poured into
         the gardens of Europe."

1925

1925 A BOOKS - NONE

1925 B SHORTER WRITINGS

1   BRETT-JAMES, NORMAN G. "Chapter V: Collinson and His Ameri-
        can Friends," in The Life of Peter Collinson. London:
        Edgar G. Dunstan, pp. 119-69.
            Uses the Bartram/Collinson correspondence to reveal the
        exchange of plants between the men, their friendship
        (which lasted for thirty-eight years) and occasional dif-
        ferences of opinion. John Bartram was "entirely untrained"
        but became "the finest botanist of his time." Collinson's
        "very great opinion of Bartram's ability" was expressed
        through a wide variety of aid (books and gifts, securing
        friends and patrons and the position of botanist to the
        king for Bartram, a constant supply of advice on many
        topics).

2   MIDDLETON, WILLIAM S. "John Bartram, Botanist," Scientific
        Monthly, XXI (July), 191-216.
            John Bartram turned to the study of botany from an in-
        terest in medicine. Quotations illustrate the exchange
        between Bartram and Collinson. Bartram's correspondence
        shows "constant inquiry into the medicinal value of the
        plants." His claim to fame for medical contributions is
        "rather insecure," but he made some significant observa-
        tions on the therapeutic use of herbs. Describes his work
        on his farm, his home, and his garden.

1928 A BOOKS - NONE

1928 B SHORTER WRITINGS

1   ANON. "The Bartrams: The Travels of William Bartram," SatR,
        IV (21 April), 786.
            Gives biographies of John and William Bartram. The Bar-
        trams influenced the English Romantic movement and belong
        to that movement. They contributed to English thought the
        image of the Indian as happy, noble savage.

2   [CADBURY, HENRY J.] "The Disownment of John Bartram," Bulle-
        tin of Friends' Historical Association, XVII (Spring),
        16-22.
            Prints a facsimile copy of the official letter of dis-
        ownment of Bartram by the Darby Monthly Meeting of Friends
        in 1758, and reproduces the transcript of the minutes of
        the Darby Meeting for the months during which his case was

(CADBURY, HENRY J.)
mentioned. Bartram's Unitarianism foreshadowed the posi-
tion of many Quakers 70 years later. Discusses his religious opinions and piety. Darlington's Memorials probably omitted many of the unorthodox and more negative
passages from Bartram's writings.

3   FAIRS, JOHN T. "How John Bartram Learned Nature's Lessons,"
in The Romance of Forgotten Men. Freeport, N. Y.: Books
for Libraries Press, pp. 24-33.
Summarizes John Bartram's life, botanical studies, work
in his garden. Quotations from William Bartram illustrate
places that John Bartram explored. Quotations from Letters
from an American Farmer describe the visit to John Bartram
and the latter's sudden conversion to botany. Explains
John Bartram's correspondence with Collinson and distinguished naturalists of the time. Describes the botanical
garden, John Bartram's "monument."

4   WHERRY, EDGAR T. "The History of the Franklin Tree, Franklinia Alatamaha," Journal of the Washington Academy of
Sciences, XVIII (19 March), 172-76.
The "Franklin tree" (Franklinia alatamaha Marshall) was
first discovered by John Bartram in 1765. William Bartram
described his second view of the tree (1773) in Travels
and named it after Franklin. Another sighting was recorded
in 1790. Since this date, the plant has never been found
growing wild. Wherry theorizes that later researchers mis-
judged the location and that the original plants were
destroyed by fire. The species survived because nursery-
men took cuttings from the tree Bartram transplanted to
his garden.

1929 A   BOOKS - NONE

1929 B   SHORTER WRITINGS

1   ANON. "An Account of the Bartram Garden, Philadelphia."
Philadelphia: Newman F. McGirr. Reprinted with revisions
from Horticulturist (JB1850.B1).
Adds a facsimile of an early broadside "Catalogue of
American trees and herbaceous plants most of which are now
growing and producing ripe seed in John Bartram's garden."

2   EXELL, A. W. "Two Eighteenth-Century American Naturalists:
John and William Bartram," Natural History Magazine, II,
50-58.

1930

      (EXELL, A. W.)
          Quotes from the correspondence of Bartram and Collinson;
reproduces a letter from Bartram to Fothergill that accompanied a shipment of snakes, plants, and "two of our large
Bull frogs, perhaps male & female, which if they come
safe and you have none of them before will be of great in-
nocent curiosity for ye King." See also (WB1929.B2).

3   P[EATTIE], D[ONALD] C. "John Bartram," in Dictionary of
American Biography, edited by Allen Johnson. Vol. I.
New York: Charles Scribner's Sons, 26-28.
          John Bartram's life and the development of his interest
in botany. Quotes Linnaeus's praise. Bartram's correspondence with Collinson tells "the success and failure of
every bulb and cutting," with "a racy loquacity." Bartram
also corresponded with many European and American scientists. Describes his journeys and praises his journals:
"Nothing missed Bartram's eye"; moreover, he had an
"intuition for unusual discoveries."

1930 A BOOKS - NONE

1930 B SHORTER WRITINGS

1   TRACY, HENRY CHESTER. American Naturists. New York: E. P.
Dutton & Co., pp. 29-35.
          Praises John Bartram's character, work, and piety. He
has received little recognition. Bartram was a "hardy and
enduring woodsman," a "pioneer and explorer," devoted
throughout his life to the study of plants, and founder of
the first botanical garden in America.

1931 A BOOKS - NONE

1931 B SHORTER WRITINGS

1   BARNHART, JOHN H. "Bartram Bibliography," Bartonia, Special
issue, supplement to no. 12 (31 December), 51-67.
          Lists, with occasional brief annotation: published
writings of John Bartram (books, papers); publications relating to John and William Bartram and the Bartram Garden;
catalogs of the Bartram Garden. Extensive list of minor
secondary sources.

2   _____. "John Bartram's First Interest in Botany," Bartonia,
Special issue, supplement to no. 12 (31 December), 35-37.

(BARNHART, JOHN H.)
According to Letters from an American Farmer, Bartram's
career as a botanist began with sudden awareness of the
intricacy of a daisy. The daisy was common in America,
although skeptics have denied its prevalence. William
Bartram's account of his father does not include but also
does not contradict the story of the daisy.

3   _____. "Significance of John Bartram's Work to Botanical and
Horticultural Knowledge," Bartonia, Special issue, supplement to no. 12 (31 December), 24-34.
John Bartram's most important work consisted in collecting American plants and introducing them into England.
Discusses the kinds and approximate number of plants sent
to England. Although he did not publish much, Bartram
also studied plants (pollination, hybridization).

4   BAXTER, SAMUEL N. "Restoration of Plants in Bartram's Garden
by the Fairmount Park Commission of Philadelphia," Bartonia, Special issue, supplement to no. 12 (31 December),
38-50.
Lists the plants found in Bartram's Garden. The garden
has been "restored" with plants known to have been grown
by Bartram.

5   BRETT-JAMES, NORMAN G. "John Bartram and His Botanic Garden,"
N&Q, CLXI (1 August), 75-76.
John Bartram deserves notice not only for starting the
first botanic garden in the New World but also because he
helped to stock many of the best-known gardens of England.
"Kew and Kenwood owe much of their initial success to Bartram and Collinson." Bartram was "one of the finest
botanists of his time," "very advanced" in religious and
political views, and differed from Collinson by being
hostile to the Indians.

6   CHESTON, MRS. EDWARD M. "Permanent Bartram Exhibition at the
Academy of Natural Sciences," Bartonia, Special issue,
supplement to no. 12 (31 December), 68.
Lists and describes some of the books and personal pos-
sessions belonging to John and William Bartram that compose
a permanent exhibit at the Academy of Natural Sciences.

7   TRUE, RODNEY H. "John Bartram's Life and Botanical Explorations," Bartonia, Special issue, supplement to no. 12 (31
December), 7-19.
Describes the journeys John Bartram undertook during a
"life of pilgrimage" dedicated to the study of American

1932

(TRUE, RODNEY H.)
  plants. Also reports on Bartram's relationships with the
  many distinguished Europeans and Americans interested in
  his discoveries.

1932 A BOOKS - NONE

1932 B SHORTER WRITINGS

1   CARDWELL, ROBERT H. "American-English Communications of
           Three Colonial Scholars, 1700-1775," Tennessee Historical
           Magazine, II (July), 227-33.
             Discusses John Bartram along with Humphry Marshall and
           Benjamin Franklin. Bartram belongs to "the class of the
           unlearned native." His "schooling" took place in his gar-
           den and his journeys. Explains the exchange of plants be-
           tween England and America. Bartram moved "into the class
           of the learned," was appointed Royal botanist, and became
           "one of the most important scholars in botanic studies and
           scientific thought in America."

2   SERRILL, WILLIAM J. "John Bartram, Botanist," The General
           Magazine and Historical Chronicle, XXXIV, 512-25.
             The bi-centennial of the founding of Bartram's Garden
           was celebrated in 1931. Biography of John Bartram, the
           founding of the garden, description and history of John
           Bartram's house. Quotes William Bartram and Crèvecoeur on
           John Bartram's virtues. Quotes Bartram's correspondence
           on his botanical work. John Bartram is not commemorated
           by any American plant. Lists Bartram's many distinguished
           friends.

1933 A BOOKS - NONE

1933 B SHORTER WRITINGS

1   JENKINS, CHARLES F. "The Historical Background of Franklin's
           Tree," PMHB, LVII (July), 193-208.
             In 1765 John and William Bartram discovered and named
           the "Franklin tree" (Franklinia alatamaha). Article in-
           cludes William's watercolor of the tree and a map of the
           location in Georgia. William again encountered the grove
           of trees in 1773 and brought back plants or seeds to Penn-
           sylvania. Since 1790, no one has seen the plant growing
           wild; hence, every Franklinia can be traced back to the
           one in the Bartram garden.

2   THATCHER, HERBERT. "Dr. Mitchell, M.D., F.R.S., of Virginia,"
        VMHB, XLI (January), 59-70.
          Quotes from a letter John Bartram wrote to Mitchell in
        1744 and notes that Mitchell visited Bartram in 1745.

1935 A BOOKS - NONE

1935 B SHORTER WRITINGS

1   ZIRKLE, CONWAY. "John Bartram," in The Beginnings of Plant
        Hybridization. Philadelphia: University of Pennsylvania
        Press, pp. 144-49.
          Records of John Bartram's experiments in plant hybridiza-
        tion are "very incomplete." He described his work in
        three letters. Only one letter, written to William Byrd,
        exists. Zirkle quotes this letter, along with a letter
        from Collinson on Bartram's experiments, and a manuscript
        in Bartram's handwriting describing his experiments with
        hybridization.

1936 A BOOKS - NONE

1936 B SHORTER WRITINGS

1   PEATTIE, DONALD C. Green Laurels: The Lives and Achievements
        of the Great Naturalists. New York: Simon and Schuster,
        pp. 189-200.
          John Bartram was a "natural botanist," the first native-
        born botanist in the New World. His science was "unlearned,
        instinctive, applied." Describes the correspondence be-
        tween Collinson and Bartram. Lists names of many other
        Bartram correspondents. Of all of Linnaeus's correspond-
        ents, Bartram furnished the most original and abundant
        materials. Tells the story of the "Franklin tree."

1937 A BOOKS - NONE

1937 B SHORTER WRITINGS

1   HARPER, FRANCIS, and ARTHUR N. LEEDS. "A Supplementary Chap-
        ter on Franklinia Alatamaha," Bartonia, no. 19 (8 March),
        1-13.
          The Franklin tree (Franklinia alatamaha Marshall) was
        discovered in 1765 in Georgia by John and William Bartram,
        and has never been discovered growing wild after 1790.

1938

(HARPER, FRANCIS...)
William Bartram reports on a spring flowering season, but
the flowering season apparently varies according to lati-
tude. Discusses evidence for locating the exact locality
of the species and its ecological distribution. Describes
"the long search" for Franklinia. Lists illustrations of
Franklinia and discusses possible causes of extinction of
the wild specimens.

1938 A BOOKS - NONE

1938 B SHORTER WRITINGS

1   CHESTON, EMILY R. John Bartram, 1699-1777; His Garden and
        His House; William Bartram, 1739-1823. Philadelphia:
        John Bartram Association.
           Biography of John Bartram, with emphasis on important
        patrons--Sir Hans Sloane, Philip Miller, Peter Collinson.
        Discusses John Bartram's correspondence with Collinson and
        others and his botanical travels. The history of the Bar-
        trams' land (with a description of the buildings); a de-
        scription and history of John Bartram's house; the history
        of the garden with attention to plants of special interest.
        Lists plants named for Bartram and his acquaintances. In-
        cludes an account of the history and work of the John
        Bartram Association.

1939 A BOOKS - NONE

1939 B SHORTER WRITINGS

1   HARPER, FRANCIS. "The Bartram Trail through the Southeastern
        States," Bulletin of the Garden Club of America, 7th ser.,
        no. 5 (September), pp. 54-64.
           Harper retraced the Bartram routes from Philadelphia
        through Virginia, the Carolinas, Georgia, Alabama, and
        Florida. He compares some of the scenes, buildings, roads,
        plants and animals he encountered with the descriptions
        supplied by the Bartrams. Bartram enthusiasts aided the
        task of retracing the routes. The discovery of a 1772 map
        followed by William Bartram has resolved questions about
        the route across Georgia and Alabama. "Perhaps the climax
        of the whole trip was the identification of the very la-
        goon where the younger Bartram had his terrific adventures
        with the alligators, and of the near-by shell mound where
        he camped!"

1940 A BOOKS

1   EARNEST, ERNEST. _John and William Bartram: Botanists and Explorers_. Philadelphia: University of Pennsylvania Press.

     John Bartram's early life, his study of botany, and the botanic garden. Bartram's friendship with Philadelphia savants (Logan, Franklin), who shared his practical and scientific interests and his rational, secular tastes. Examines the Bartram/Collinson friendship, and Bartram's important role in gardening. Bartram's travels and the journals and letters which report them. His "religion of nature," based on the Enlightenment belief in order. Recognition and awards during his lifetime and afterwards. Bartram "became one of the recognized figures in the intellectual life of the age."

1940 B SHORTER WRITINGS - NONE

1944 A BOOKS - NONE

1944 B SHORTER WRITINGS

1   HARPER, FRANCIS. "Introduction," _Diary of a Journey through the Carolinas, Georgia, and Florida, 1765-66_, by John Bartram, edited by Francis Harper. _Transactions of the American Philosophical Society_, n.s. XXXIII (December), 1-12.

     Gives a selected bibliography of John Bartram (primarily of biographical works). Discusses the hardships of the journey, and supplies a list of Bartram's other journeys. Describes the manuscript diary of 1765-66 and notes previously published portions. Reports on investigations of the Bartram routes. Discusses editorial features of the _Diary_. Bartram's work has "scarcely a single literary flourish" and does not take full advantage of his unique opportunity. But it is valuable as a picture of the American wilderness when it was "primeval and unspoiled."

2   _____. "Literature Cited," in _Diary of a Journey through the Carolinas, Georgia, and Florida, 1765-1766_, by John Bartram, edited by Francis Harper. _Transactions of the American Philosophical Society_, n.s. XXXIII (December), 108-111.

     Bibliography of editions and reprints of John and William Bartram's works, secondary sources on John Bartram, and sources that provide information to clarify or supplement John Bartram's writings.

1949

1949 A BOOKS - NONE

1949 B SHORTER WRITINGS

1   TOLLES, FREDERICK B. "Writers of the Middle Colonies," in
       Literary History of the United States, edited by Robert E.
       Spiller, et al. Vol. I. New York: Macmillan Co., 91.
          Bartram was "a tireless collector" of botanical speci-
       mens. His "laconic" style combined the Quaker tradition
       of plain speech with the search for scientific precision.
       Even in exotic Florida "the taciturn Quaker naturalist,
       distrustful of emotion, permitted himself only a restrained
       scientific curiosity."

1954 A BOOKS

1   HERBST, JOSEPHINE. New Green World. New York: Hastings
       House.
          A biography of John Bartram. Detailed use of the Bartram
       letters, particularly those to Collinson, to elucidate
       Bartram's life, work, and character, and the age in which
       he lived. "The correspondence between Collinson and Bar-
       tram was a long duet of discovery, rapture and a dash of
       vinegar when it came to disputed questions." Turns Bar-
       tram's journals into well-written literary accounts of his
       journeys. Continual praise for John Bartram and his fellow
       eighteenth-century scientists as "whole men," from whose
       work grew "emotions...profoundly wrapped in wonder of the
       creation."

1954 B SHORTER WRITINGS

1   LEARY, LEWIS. "Bartram, John," in Articles on American
       Literature, 1900-1950. Durham, N.C.: Duke University
       Press, p. 18.
          Lists journal articles on John Bartram from 1900-1950.

1955 A BOOKS - NONE

1955 B SHORTER WRITINGS

1   WEST, FRANCIS D. "John Bartram and Slavery," The South Caro-
       lina Historical Magazine, LVI (April), 115-19.
          In the (generally accepted) account of John Bartram in Let-
       ters from an American Farmer, he has freed his slaves and
       gives them the privileges of white men. The information is

(WEST, FRANCIS D.)
inaccurate, because Bartram had already turned over most of
his property to his sons by the date specified. Moreover,
a letter from John Bartram to William Bartram demonstrates
a "belief in slavery," for he expresses "no more considera-
tion" for the slaves than for the supplies he was sending
his son.

1956 A BOOKS - NONE

1956 B SHORTER WRITINGS

1   BELL, MALCOLM, JR. "Eye Witnesses to a Vanished America,"
        GaR, X (Spring), 13-23.
            John Bartram was the first native-born naturalist. As
        Royal botanist he set out on a hazardous trip in 1765. He
        was fascinated by the Savannah River valley. Much of what
        he described in his journal remains the same today. See
        also (WB1956.B1).

2   WEST, FRANCIS D. "John Bartram and the American Philosophical
        Society," Pennsylvania History, XXIII (October), 463-66.
            In a 1739 letter to Collinson, John Bartram proposes an
        academy or society to study natural science. The letter
        provides evidence that Bartram first proposed the idea of
        the American Philosophical Society. Bartram's letters
        from 1744 show his connection with the Society in its
        nativity.

1957 A BOOKS - NONE

1957 B SHORTER WRITINGS

1   BRADFORD, ROBERT W. "John Bartram," in "Journey into Nature:
        American Nature Writing, 1733-1860." Ph.D. dissertation,
        Syracuse University, pp. 47-60.
            Observations is "the almost incoherent jottings of a
        traveler whose only apparent purpose was to inform, clearly
        and accurately." Bartram was a "classical Linnean
        traveler" searching with passionate interest for new
        species. Observations shows an interest in Indian habits
        and ecological relationships. The work shows "a habit of
        seeing the natural world according to some pattern of
        aesthetics" (especially with regard to "romantic"
        scenery).

1958

2   CADBURY, B. BARTRAM. "Foreword," in John and William Bar-
     tram's America: Selections from the Writings of the Phila-
     delphia Naturalists, edited by Helen Gere Cruickshank.
     New York: Devin-Adair Company, pp. v-vi.
         John and William Bartram were important in the develop-
     ment of American science. John Bartram's scant writing is
     "rather labored." William Bartram took over the task of
     reporting on their work and did so with realism and humor.
     William's work has never been as well known in America as
     in other countries. The Bartrams were "intrepid travel-
     lers" who faced many dangers.

3   CRUICKSHANK, HELEN GERE. "Introduction," in John and William
     Bartram's America: Selections from the Writings of the
     Philadelphia Naturalists, edited by Helen Gere Cruickshank.
     New York: The Devin-Adair Company, pp. xi-xix.
         The Bartrams saw the American wilderness "with the eyes
     of great botanists, of philosophers, explorers, historians,
     and ecologists." John Bartram's journals were "blunt and
     brief as a captain's log." William Bartram's entries were
     "vivid and joyous." John Bartram's personality was more
     forceful; William Bartram had "a poet's appreciation" for
     nature. Travels furnishes "the first genuinely artistic"
     picture of the Southeast.

4   PRINCE, WINIFRED NOTMAN. "John Bartram in the Cedar Swamps,"
     PMHB, LXXXI (January), 86-88.
         To determine the correct classification of American
     evergreens, Collinson asked John Bartram to collect speci-
     mens of trees. In 1736 Bartram did so. His account of
     the trip is quoted in a letter of Collinson's. Bartram's
     description of the plants led to classification of the
     white as a true cedar and the red as not a cedar.

5   WEST, FRANCIS D. "Sweden Honors John Bartram," PMHB, LXXXI
     (January), 88-90.
         In 1769, John Bartram was elected a member of the Royal
     Academy of Sciences of Stockholm.

1958 A   BOOKS - NONE

1958 B   SHORTER WRITINGS

1   EDELSTEIN, J. M. "America's First Native Botanists," The
     Library of Congress Quarterly Journal of Current Acquisi-
     tions, XV (February), 51-59.

(EDELSTEIN, J. M.)
  Discusses the complete collection of early editions of
major works by John and William Bartram now owned by the
Library of Congress. Summarizes their lives, gives background on their travels, and describes and quotes their
works. John Bartram's Observations is an "exciting and
highly readable book ... one of the most charming early
travel narratives by an American." In Travels, William
Bartram redescribed much that his father had written of in
his Journal; the description of fountains that influenced
Coleridge uses language similar to John Bartram's.

2   HARPER, FRANCIS. "References: Literature (Including Manu-
     scripts)," in The Travels of William Bartram: Naturalist's
     Edition, edited by Francis Harper. New Haven: Yale Uni-
     versity Press, pp. 668-89.
       Bibliography of primary sources on John and William
     Bartram (editions, reprints, translations, manuscripts),
     secondary sources on them (especially on their scientific
     achievements), works useful in clarifying and supplementing
     their writings.

3   PRIOR, MARY BARBOT. "Letters of Martha Logan to John Bartram,
     1760-1763," The South Carolina Historical Magazine, LIX
     (January), 38-46.
       Martha Logan "carried on a lively exchange of letters and
     seeds with John Bartram." Seven of her letters (mostly
     concerned with information on seeds and plants) are quoted.

4   WEST, FRANCIS D. "John Bartram: Geologist," The Bulletin of
     Friends'Historical Association, XLVII (Spring), 35-38.
       John Bartram has probably never been credited with being
     the "first American-born geologist." He suggested theories
     usually credited to other scientists (theories that streams
     eroded their valleys, that America had been under water,
     that cold latitudes formerly had hot climates). Most im-
     portantly, more than a century before such work was under-
     taken, he proposed a geological survey based upon the use
     of extensive drilling.

1959 A   BOOKS - NONE

1959 B   SHORTER WRITINGS

1   BELL, WHITFIELD J., JR. and RALPH L. KETCHAM. "A Tribute to
     John Bartram, with a Note on Jacob Engelbrecht," PMHB,
     LXXXIII (October), 446-51.

1963

(BELL, WHITFIELD J., JR....)
   Quotes an imitation of Horace's Ode 22 which praises
John Bartram. The authors attribute this verse to Joseph
Breintnall. The verses were wrongly attributed to Franklin
by James Madison, who later learned that the handwriting
was not Franklin's.

1963 A BOOKS

1   SUTTON, ANN, and MYRON SUTTON. Exploring with the Bartrams.
       Eau Claire, Wis.: E. M. S. Hale Company.
          Biography of John and William Bartram for children.
       Based on the Bartrams' own writings. Emphasizes their ex-
       ploration of the American wilderness. Illustrations in-
       clude maps, photographs, and drawings by William Bartram.

1963 B SHORTER WRITINGS - NONE

1966 A BOOKS - NONE

1966 B SHORTER WRITINGS

1   ANON. "Foreword," in Travels in Pensilvania and Canada, by
       John Bartram. Ann Arbor, Mich.: University Microfilms,
       Inc.
          The volume reprints Observations. John Bartram's work
       gives one of the best descriptions of the American wilder-
       ness in mid-eighteenth century. Bartram's biography.
       His remarks on the Indians are particularly interesting.

1967 A BOOKS - NONE

1967 B SHORTER WRITINGS

1   EWAN, JOSEPH. "Introduction," in Memorials of John Bartram
       and Humphry Marshall, edited by William Darlington. New
       York: Hafner Publishing Co., pp. v-xiv.
          Darlington's Memorials is "probably the most frequently
       cited book today dealing with eighteenth-century botanical
       history in the American Colonies." Ewan quotes praise of
       the value of the book and criticism of Darlington's "edi-
       torial liberties" with the letters. Provides a bibliog-
       raphy for further information on the people mentioned in
       the letters. Includes a chronology of John Bartram's life
       and a brief bibliography on him.

1968 A   BOOKS - NONE

1968 B   SHORTER WRITINGS

1   EWAN, JOSEPH.   "Bibliographic References," in William Bartram:
        Botanical and Zoological Drawings, 1756-1788, edited by
        Joseph Ewan.   Philadelphia: American Philosophical Society,
        pp. 168-72.
                Bibliography of manuscripts and published works by John
        and William Bartram, secondary sources (including manu-
        scripts) supplying information on them, and general informa-
        tion on topics related to their work, particularly in
        science and ethnology.

2   WILSON, DAVID S.   "Chapter 4:   John Bartram," in "The Streaks
        of the Tulip: The Literary Aspects of Eighteenth-Century
        American Natural Philosophy."   Ph.D. dissertation, Uni-
        versity of Minnesota, pp. 125-75.
                Bartram has been highly praised as scientist but neglected
        as writer.   Excerpts from Bartram's travel journals and
        letters prove he produced "fragments which so wed content
        and style as to qualify as art."   These are often portraits
        of particular specimens or descriptions of active scenes.
        Virtuosi like Bartram and Jonathan Carver used plain speech
        in their nature writing.   Examines the structure of Obser-
        vations.   Contrasts Bartram with Gilbert White.

1969 A   BOOKS - NONE

1969 B   SHORTER WRITINGS

1   DAVIS, RICHARD B.   "John Bartram (1700?-1768)," in American
        Literature through Bryant, 1585-1830.   New York: Appleton-
        Century-Crofts, p. 49.
                Short list of selected primary and secondary sources.

2   SULLIVAN, WILLIAM J.   "Chapter I: John Bartram: A Citizen of
        the New World," in "Towards Romanticism: A Study of
        William Bartram."   Ph.D. dissertation, University of Utah,
        pp. 7-21.
                Unlike the "romantic" William Bartram, John Bartram was
        "in many ways the epitome of the Enlightenment."   He was
        "practical," interested in science, a deist and secular-
        minded, and of a highly rationalistic temperament, quali-
        ties appropriate to the Age of Reason.   He belonged to
        illustrious scientific circles, was involved in the affairs
        of Philadelphia (the capital of the "Age of Reason" in the

1970

(SULLIVAN, WILLIAM J.)
colonies), and in general was "completely in step with the
dominant intellectual spirit as well as the scientific
spirit of his age."

1970 A BOOKS - NONE

1970 B SHORTER WRITINGS

1   LEARY, LEWIS. "Bartram, John," in Articles on American
         Literature, 1950-1967. Durham, N.C.: Duke University
         Press, p. 25.
              Lists journal articles on John Bartram from 1950-1967.

1972 A BOOKS - NONE

1972 B SHORTER WRITINGS

1   MEDEIROS, PATRICIA M. "John Bartram," in "The Literature of
         Travel of Eighteenth-Century America." Ph.D. dissertation,
         University of Massachusetts, pp. 179-93.
              The style of John Bartram's Diary, which recounts his
         trip to Florida, is plain, intended largely to record in-
         formation. Much of the book is written almost as notes
         which were formed into rudimentary sentences in the part
         that was published. The persona of the book is self-
         effacing; his outstanding characteristic is practicality.
         He does not show extreme scientific detachment, neverthe-
         less, because he typically admires what he sees. The one
         outstanding theme is the "theme of measurement ... meas-
         uring and charting to reduce the unknown to knowable
         quantities."

1973 A BOOKS - NONE

1973 B SHORTER WRITINGS

1   BELL, WHITFIELD J., JR. "Introduction," in A Journey from
         Pennsylvania to Onondaga in 1743, by John Bartram, Lewis
         Evans [and] Conrad Weiser. Barre, Mass.: Imprint Society,
         pp. 7-18.
              As representative of Pennsylvania, John Bartram accom-
         panied Conrad Weiser, Lewis Evans, and an Indian guide to
         an Iroquois Council. Introduces the four men and gives a
         synopsis of events on the journey. Bartram's journal of

1974

(BELL, WHITFIELD J., JR.)
the trip is significant because of his observations on
natural history, and on the Indians, and his thoughts on
the conflict between the French and British.

1974 A   BOOKS - NONE

1974 B   SHORTER WRITINGS

1   SPILLER, ROBERT E., et al., eds. "John and William Bartram,"
        in Literary History of the United States: Bibliography.
        4th ed., rev. New York: Macmillan Co., pp. 398-99, 874-
        75, 1147-48.
           Lists separate works, collected works, primary sources,
        bibliography, selected biographical and critical works.

Writings About William Bartram, 1792 - 1974

1792 A   BOOKS - NONE

1792 B   SHORTER WRITINGS

1   ANON. "Monthly Review of New American Books: Travels
        through North and South Carolina, East and West Florida
        &c., &c.," Massachusetts Magazine, or, Monthly Museum, IV
        (November), 686-87.
           Amateurs of natural science will be "highly gratified"
        by Travels. Bartram's botanical researches are "copious,"
        he accurately describes new species of animals, and gives
        minute attention to the Indians. He is "rather too luxuri-
        ant and florid," but these trivial faults result from his
        poetical imagination, and are countered by his piety and
        morality. Quotes a long extract on the Indians.

2   ANON. "Travels through North and South Carolina," The Univer-
        sal Asylum and Columbian Magazine, I (March, April), 195-97,
        255-67.
           Traces William Bartram's journey by summarizing and
        quoting liberally from Travels. Bartram probably "magni-
        fies the virtue" of the Indians. The merits of Travels
        "entitle the author to a respectable place among those, who
        have devoted their time and talents to the improvement of
        natural science." Bartram should have omitted information
        on plants which are not remarkable or peculiar to the
        country and also omitted "many rhapsodical effusions." The
        style is "very incorrect and disgustingly pompous." The
        faults, however, are less significant than the "many useful
        and various facts."

1793 A   BOOKS - NONE

1793 B   SHORTER WRITINGS

1   ANON. "New Books: Travels through North and South Carolina,"
        The Scots Magazine, LV (January), 17-23.

1794

(ANON.)
John Bartram, a botanical traveler and botanist to the king, receives "very respectful mention" in Letters from an American Farmer. William Bartram searched the South for rare and useful productions of nature at the request of Dr. Fothergill of London. Provides a sample of the hazards and perils he met. "He makes us shudder in describing one of his evening disturbances" by the alligators.

2   N[OVTHOUCK]. "Bartram's Travels," The Monthly Review; or, Literary Journal, X (January, April), 13-22, 130-38.
Most of this review of Travels consists of long extracts about Bartram's dangers among the Indians and "that horrible monster, the American alligator, or crocodile." Bartram's praise of the Indians cannot be trusted, for he also reports on their uncivilized behavior. Bartram is "an amusing and intelligent observer," but his language is likely to be "somewhat too luxuriant and poetical."

3   ZIMMERMAN, EBERHARD A. W. "Vorrede des Uebersetzers," in William Bartrams Reisen durch Nord- und Süd-Karolina, Georgien, Ost- und West-Florida, das Gebiet der Tscherokesen, Krihks und Tschaktahs, nebst Umständlichen Nachrichten von dem Einwohnern, dem Boden und den Naturprodukten dieser Wenig Bekannten Grossen Länder. Translated by E. A. W. Zimmermann. Berlin: Vossichen Buchhandlung, pp. iii-x.
Travels is one of the most instructive works of our time. Bartram reports on land which is so little known that it is depicted only in general on the maps. Bartram describes little-known Indians, and a number of new plants and animals. The style is often verbose and bombastic. Zimmerman has made the translation "more readable" by eliminating the superfluous.

1794 A BOOKS - NONE

1794 B SHORTER WRITINGS

1   MEYER, FRIEDRICH. "Neue Thiere aus William Bertrams Reisen, durch Nord- und Südcarolina," Zoologische Annalen, I, 283-98.
Lists and describes animals (for instance, the "goldfish," North American wood rat, savannah crane, "Vultur sacra") that Bartram described in Travels.

2   PASTEUR, JEAN D. Reizen door Noord- en Zuid-Carolina, Georgia, Oost- en West-Florida; de Landen der Cherokees, der

(PASTEUR, JEAN D.)
  Muscogulges, of het Creek Bondgenootschop en het Land der
  Chactaws. Translated by Jean David Pasteur. Vol. I.
  Haarlem, Netherlands: Francois Bohn.
    Lengthy introduction to Dutch translation of Travels.
  Focuses on William Bartram's report on American flora and
  fauna and the Indians and his theories with regard to
  natural history and the Indian. Bartram believes the life
  principle is more similar in plants and animals than is
  generally believed. Bartram has seen many examples of true
  parent-child love and true fidelity in animals. Bartram
  lived among the Indians to see if the accusation they were
  unfit for civilization was untrue. He advises the govern-
  ment to send men to live among them to form opinions on
  appropriate legislation and possible union with the Indians.

1799 A BOOKS - NONE

1799 B SHORTER WRITINGS

1   ANON. "Voyage dans les Parties du Sud de l'Amérique Septen-
         trionale," La Clef du Cabinet des Souverains, no. 733
         (January-February), p. 6267.
           Review of the French translation of Travels (1799). The
         principal object of the book is natural history, but it
         should interest more than the learned. Soil, climate,
         plants and animals are observed. Several are new; all are
         interesting. The reader learns with pleasure about croco-
         diles, and ephemera. Bartram never describes nature with
         didactic dryness or with the exaggerated enthusiasm of
         certain travellers. The translation is better than most;
         the style is correct and does not lack elegance.

1827 A BOOKS - NONE

1827 B SHORTER WRITINGS

1   ANON. "Florida," American Quarterly Review, II (September),
         226.
           Travels contains "a great number of most interesting
         facts and observations." Regrets Bartram's lack of "sys-
         tematic precision" and frequent "exclamatory admiration at
         the beauties and wonders of Nature." "His rambling mode of
         writing, is rendered fatiguing and unsatisfactory by a
         minute record of his reflections, rather than his observa-
         tions." The book "will always be referred to as conveying

1828

(ANON.)
a good general idea of the counties through which he
passed." "A very entertaining and useful treatise containing about half the number of pages, might be <u>digested</u> from
his volume."

1828 A BOOKS - NONE

1828 B SHORTER WRITINGS

1   ORD, GEORGE. <u>Sketch of the Life of Alexander Wilson</u>. Phila-
       delphia: Harrison Hall, pp. xxii-xxiii.
          Wilson's "uncommon friendship" with Bartram lasted until
       death. Bartram lent Wilson books, encouraged his study of
       nature and generally functioned as "friend and instructor."
       Ord's sketch prints many letters from Wilson to Bartram.

1831 A BOOKS - NONE

1831 B SHORTER WRITINGS

1   MEASE, JAMES. "Bartram's Botanic Garden on the Schuylkill,
       near Philadelphia," <u>Gardener's Magazine, and Register of
       Rural and Domestic Improvement</u>, VII (December), 665-66.
          William Bartram was "the counterpart of his father in
       moral excellence, amiability, and love of natural history,
       and his superior in science." Most of the article is de-
       voted to John Bartram and the Bartram Garden (JB1831.B1).

1832 A BOOKS - NONE

1832 B SHORTER WRITINGS

1   [ORD, GEORGE.] "Biographical Sketch of William Bartram,"
       <u>Cabinet of Natural History and Rural Sports, with Illustra-
       tions</u>, II, i-viii.
          Reproduces a portrait of William Bartram, "a correct
       likeness ... and the only engraved one ever given to the
       American public." In the past, Bartram's "fame extended
       to both continents; in his sphere, he was one of the most
       eminent men of America ..." Sketches the events of Bar-
       tram's life. Declares he volunteered to help repel an ex-
       pected British invasion of the South in 1776. Quotes at
       length from <u>Travels</u>, focusing on Bartram's adventures with
       the alligators (which afterwards disturbed his sleep with

(ORD, GEORGE)
    "violent and hideous dreams"). Discusses Bartram's aid to
    Wilson and other naturalists. William Bartram "saw nothing
    but mildness and harmony" in all of nature's works.
    Reprinted as American Philosophical Society Pamphlet V.
    (WB1832.B2); See also (JB1832.B2).

2   _____. "Biographical Sketch of William Bartram with Portrait,"
    American Philosophical Society Pamphlet V, 1166.
      Reprinted from Cabinet of Natural History and Rural
    Sports (WB1832.B1).

1836 A BOOKS - NONE

1836 B SHORTER WRITINGS

1   COLERIDGE, SAMUEL TAYLOR. Specimens of the Table Talk of
    Samuel Taylor Coleridge. 2nd ed. London: John Murray,
    p. 33.
      "The latest book of travels I know, written in the spirit
    of the old travellers, is Bartram's account of his tour in
    the Floridas. It is a work of high merit in every way."

1853 A BOOKS - NONE

1853 B SHORTER WRITINGS

1   SQUIER, E. G. "Prefatory Note," in Observations on the Creek
    and Cherokee Indians, 1789, by William Bartram. Transac-
    tions of the American Ethnological Society, III, 3-7.
      Introduces the first publication of a manuscript written
    by William Bartram (probably in response to questions
    posed by B. S. Barton) on the Indians of Florida and the
    earthworks found near the Gulf of Mexico. Bartram "was a
    close accurate and conscientious observer." His descrip-
    tion of the Indians is a valuable contribution to archae-
    ology and ethnology.

1855 A BOOKS - NONE

1855 B SHORTER WRITINGS

1   DUYCKINCK, EVERT A., and GEORGE L. DUYCKINCK. "William Bar-
    tram," in Cyclopaedia of American Literature. Vol. I.
    New York: Charles Scribner. Reprinted. Detroit: Gale
    Research Company, 1965, 233-38.

1859

(DUYCKINCK, EVERT A. ...)
Praises Bartram's Travels because of his "simple love of
nature and vivacity...freshness...natural emotion...simple
and pure tastes...lively gratification of the senses and
emotions." "All his faculties are alive in his book,
whether he describes a tree, a fish, a bird, beast, Indian,
or hospitable planter." Bartram finds "fragrance, vitality,
and health" everywhere in the natural world. His accounts
of the Southern Indians show them as possessing many ad-
mirable qualities. Sketches Bartram's life. He assisted
Wilson. The article includes long extracts from Travels.

1859 A BOOKS - NONE

1859 B SHORTER WRITINGS

1   ALLIBONE, SAMUEL A. "Bartram, William," in A Critical Dic-
        tionary of English Literature and British and American
        Authors. Vol. I. Philadelphia: J. B. Lippincott Company.
        Reprinted. Detroit: Gale Research Co., 1965, 137.
            Bartram "inherited the botanical zeal" of his father.
        Reports on his travels in Florida. Travels is "a delight-
        ful specimen" of the nature lover's enthusiasm for the
        beauty and wonder of the world.

2   SIMPSON, HENRY. "William Bartram," in The Lives of Eminent
        Philadelphians, Now Deceased. Philadelphia: W. Brother-
        head, pp. 36-37.
            Dr. Fothergill employed William Bartram to examine the
        natural productions of the Southeast. Bartram also com-
        piled the most complete table of American ornithology be-
        fore Wilson and helped the latter prepare his book. Lists
        William Bartram's published works.

1860 A BOOKS - NONE

1860 B SHORTER WRITINGS

1   L[IPPINCOTT, JAMES S.] "Sketches of Philadelphia Botanists:
        John and William Bartram and Humphrey Marshall," Gardener's
        Monthly and Horticulturist, II (September), 271-73.
            Brief account of William Bartram's life. Travels is
        "distinguished for its simple love of nature and its
        vivacity." Quotes the Duyckincks' and Coleridge's praise
        of Travels. William Bartram prepared a list of birds and
        helped Wilson. See also (JB1860.B2).

1864 A   BOOKS - NONE

1864 B   SHORTER WRITINGS

1   TUCKERMAN, HENRY T. <u>America</u> <u>and</u> <u>Her</u> <u>Commentators</u>: <u>With</u> <u>a</u>
      <u>Critical</u> <u>Sketch</u> <u>of</u> <u>Travel</u> <u>in</u> <u>the</u> <u>United</u> <u>States</u>. New York:
      Charles Scribner, pp. 382-85.
           Quotes Coleridge's praise of <u>Travels</u>. William Bartram's
      style is "more finished...more fluent and glowing" than
      his father's. Cites some of Bartram's "fresh and sympa-
      thetic description..." "Curiously do touches of pedantry
      alternate with those of simplicity; the matter-of-fact tone
      of Robinson Crusoe, and the grave didactics of Rasselas;
      a scientific statement after the manner of Humboldt, and
      an anecdote or interview in the style of Boswell."

1869 A   BOOKS - NONE

1869 B   SHORTER WRITINGS

1   L., J. H.   "Bartram's Diary," <u>Gardener's</u> <u>Monthly</u> <u>and</u> <u>Horticul-</u>
      <u>turist</u>, XI (May), 132-33.
           Presents extracts from "the precious memoranda of dear
      old William Bartram." Bartram's diary consists of nearly
      ten years (1802-1822) of almost daily notes, largely re-
      ports on the weather, the arrival and departure of birds,
      the appearance of insects. The almost complete absence of
      "thermometrical notes" deprives the notes of much of the
      value they could have for comparison with later observa-
      tions. The diary demonstrates the patience and close
      attention Bartram gave to nature.

1875 A   BOOKS - NONE

1875 B   SHORTER WRITINGS

1   COUES, ELLIOTT.   "Fasti Ornithologiae Redivivi--No. I.
      Bartram's Travels," <u>Proceedings</u> <u>of</u> <u>Philadelphia</u> <u>Academy</u> <u>of</u>
      <u>Natural</u> <u>Sciences</u>, XXXIV, 338-58.
           Because William Bartram has been suspected of the "crime"
      of "polynomialism," he has not received his due with regard
      to nomenclature. But Bartram was "effectually, systemati-
      cally, and on principle binomial, occasionally lapsing."
      In <u>Travels</u> Bartram treats "every one of his species with
      description, diagnosis, or definition, and left no doubt
      of his meaning in the majority of cases." "Such of his

1876

(COUES, ELLIOTT)
    species as are binomially named and fully identified must
    take their rightful place ... and those names which are
    found to possess the quality of priority must be adopted."

1876 A BOOKS - NONE

1876 B SHORTER WRITINGS

1   ALLEN, J. A. "Bartramian Names Again: an Explanation,"
        American Naturalist, X (March), 176-77.
            If Coues (WB1876.B3) had insisted on recognition of only
        those Bartramian names really identifiable by Bartram's
        descriptions, Allen would agree with him. But Coues con-
        siders "vague references to species" as descriptions. Bar-
        tram not only observed variation of size in animals from
        different localities but also "raised the inquiry whether
        these differences be not the result of...environment."

2   _____. "The Availability of Certain Bartramian Names in Or-
        nithology," American Naturalist, X (January), 21-29.
            Reply to Coues' attempt to revive some of William Bar-
        tram's names of birds (WB1875.B1). Bartram has already re-
        ceived enough recognition. In most cases, Bartram does not
        really describe the bird. Thirty-six out of 215 names are
        not binomials. Includes a list of Bartramian names Coues
        wishes to be used, with critical remarks on them. Allen
        suggests that Bartram be given credit for "priority in the
        discovery of the geographical law of variation in size in
        American mammals."

3   COUES, ELLIOTT. "Reply to Mr. J. A. Allen's 'Availability of
        Certain Bartramian Names in Ornithology,'" American Natur-
        alist, X (February), 98-102.
            Allen himself (WB1876.B2) admits Coues' major point:
        Bartram's "identifiable, described, and binomially named
        species" are entitled to recognition. The only real dis-
        agreement between the two men stems from the fact that
        Allen was not able to identify as many of Bartram's species
        as Coues. Coues criticizes Allen for devaluing Bartram as
        an ornithologist and binomialist. Coues declares Bartram
        did not discover the law of geographical variation.

1884 A BOOKS - NONE

1884 B SHORTER WRITINGS

1 CARLYLE, THOMAS, and RALPH WALDO EMERSON. The Correspondence
   of Thomas Carlyle and Ralph Waldo Emerson, 1834-1872.
   Vol. II. Boston: Houghton Mifflin and Co., p. 198.
     In 1851 Carlyle wrote the following to Emerson: "Do you
   know Bartram's Travels? This is of the Seventies (1770)
   or so; treats of Florida chiefly, has a wondrous kind of
   floundering eloquence in it; and has also grown immeasur-
   ably old. All American libraries ought to provide themselves with that kind of book; and keep them as a kind of
   biblical article."

1891 A BOOKS - NONE

1891 B SHORTER WRITINGS

1 ANON. "The Bartram Library," Philadelphia Public Ledger
   (11 September), p. 6.
     The remains of John Bartram's library, books belonging
   to William Bartram and other members of the Bartram family,
   and various family relics have been donated to the Historical Society of Pennsylvania. The collection (which
   includes many rare books) totals about 100 volumes. Lists
   specific books (among them, William Bartram's own copy of
   Travels).

1892 A BOOKS - NONE

1892 B SHORTER WRITINGS

1 [YOUMANS, WILLIAM J.] "A Portrait of William Bartram,"
   Popular Science Monthly, XLI (August), 561-62.
     The engraved portrait of William Bartram used for the
   frontispiece to J. and T. Dougherty's Cabinet of Natural
   History and American Rural Sports (Volume II, 1832) is considered authentic. See also (WB1832.B1).

2 _____. "Sketch of John and William Bartram," Popular Science
   Monthly, XL (April), 827-39.
     Brief summary of William Bartram's life and travels.
   William made many contributions to the natural history of
   the Southeast and also made the most complete list of
   American birds before Wilson. Most of the article deals
   with John Bartram (JB1892.B1).

1896

1896 A   BOOKS - NONE

1896 B   SHORTER WRITINGS

1   YOUMANS, WILLIAM J.   "John Bartram, 1699-1777, and William
          Bartram, 1739-1823," in Pioneers of Science in America.
          New York: Appleton and Co. Reprinted. Ann Arbor, Mich.:
          University Microfilms, 1965, pp. 24-39.
            Brief account of William Bartram's life, scientific
          studies, and writings. "His botanical labors brought to
          light many interesting plants not previously known," and
          he contributed to ornithology by his own list of birds and
          by aiding Wilson. Most of the article deals with John
          Bartram (JB1896.B4).

1897 A   BOOKS - NONE

1897 B   SHORTER WRITINGS

1   ANON. "Bartram, William," in The National Cyclopaedia of
          American Biography, Being the History of the United States.
          Vol. VII. New York: J. T. White and Company. Reprinted.
          Ann Arbor, Mich.: University Microfilms, 1967, pp. 154-55.
            William Bartram was employed by Dr. Fothergill to explore
          the Southeast, studying and collecting natural products.
          Notes the publication of Travels. "The illustrations in
          his [sic] Elements of Botany were drawn by his own hand and
          many of the most curious and beautiful plants of North
          America were there depicted for the first time."

1899 A   BOOKS - NONE

1899 B   SHORTER WRITINGS

1   COUES, ELLIOTT. "The Finishing Stroke to Bartram," The Auk:
          A Quarterly Journal of Ornithology, XVI (January), 83-84.
            "I have changed not and see no reason to change" the de-
          fense of Bartram as "a binomial author who sometimes
          lapses, and whose identifiable binomials which rest upon
          description are available in our nomenclature." Discusses
          names of specific birds.

2   HARSHBERGER, JOHN W. "William Bartram," in The Botanists of
          Philadelphia and Their Work. Philadelphia: T. C. Davis,
          pp. 86-88.

(HARSHBERGER, JOHN W.)
William Bartram was probably the first botanist to visit the southern portion of the Alleghenies. Gives a brief account of the itinerary of Travels (a "well-known and interesting book"). Bartram also published the "most complete and correct" list of American birds before Wilson's work. Most of the plates of B. S. Barton's Elements of Botany (1803) were engraved from original drawings by Bartram.

1901 A BOOKS - NONE

1901 B SHORTER WRITINGS

1   MOHR, CHARLES T. "History of the Earlier Botanical Explorations of Alabama. William Bartram," Contributions from the United States National Herbarium, VI (31 July), 13-15.
William Bartram was the first to describe Alabama flora. Traces his journey through the state, describing his plant discoveries and descriptions, and his account of the topography.

1902 A BOOKS - NONE

1902 B SHORTER WRITINGS

1   [NITZSCHE, GEORGE E.] "The Bartram Memorial Library," Old Pennsylvania Weekly Review, I (5 December), 1.
The Bartram Memorial Library at the University of Pennsylvania was begun by the Bartram Association. Efforts are being made to make it a good collection of American botanical books, including books from 1750 to 1850. Lists specific additions to the library.

1903 A BOOKS - NONE

1903 B SHORTER WRITINGS

1   BÉDIER, CHARLES M. J. Études Critiques. Paris: Librairie Armand Colin, pp. 199-203, 206-19, 224-26, 249-58, 264, 265, 269, 271, 273, 277, 278, 283-87, 290.
Extensive quotation of parallel passages from Travels and Chateaubriand's works show William Bartram's strong influence on the latter.

1905

1905 A BOOKS - NONE

1905 B SHORTER WRITINGS

1   COOPER, LANE. "Bartram Redivivus?" The Nation, LXXX (23
            February), 152.
                Suggests the need for reprinting Travels. Lists the
            editions and translations of Travels and notes several
            versions of it in Swedish ("no doubt in consequence of the
            friendly relationship between Bartram and the successors
            of Linnaeus"). Although scientists have always appreciated
            the book, it is rare and has been neglected by historians
            of literature. Travels is important because it influenced
            Coleridge, Wordsworth, Chateaubriand and other writers.

2   _____. "Wordsworth Sources," The Athenaeum Journal, no. 4043
            (22 April), 498-500.
                Presents passages from Wordsworth, in particular The
            Prelude and "Ruth," to prove Wordsworth was greatly influ-
            enced by the scenery and diction of Travels. Wordsworth's
            pantheism resembles Bartram's "immanent spirit." The poet,
            however, also disapproved of the lushness of Bartram's
            sub-tropical world and its effect on men.

3   STONE, WITMER. "Some Early American Ornithologists: II.
            William Bartram," Bird Lore, VII (June), 162-64.
                Title varies; also called Audubon Magazine. Sketch of
            William Bartram's life. Travels includes accounts of birds
            and a list of nomenclature of the birds he knew from Penn-
            sylvania to Florida. This list "was a landmark in the
            progress of American ornithology, the next in importance
            to the work of Catesby and the first ornithological con-
            tribution worthy of the name written by a native American."
            Quotes records of birds from William Bartram's diary. His
            "profound knowledge and the assistance it enabled him to
            offer to others" (in particular, Thomas Say, B. S. Barton,
            and Alexander Wilson) did more for ornithology than his
            list.

1906 A BOOKS - NONE

1906 B SHORTER WRITINGS

1   BRITTEN, JAMES. "Bibliographical Notes. XXXVIII. John
            Bartram's Travels," Journal of Botany, British and Foreign,
            XLIV (June), 213, 214.
                Lists biographical data, selected primary and secondary
            sources.

2   COLERIDGE, ERNEST H. "Coleridge, Wordsworth, and the American
     Botanist William Bartram," Transactions of the Royal So-
     ciety of Literature, 2d ser. XXVII, 69-92.
        Extracts from Travels in a private notebook of Coleridge's
     ("Gulch Memorandum Book") show Coleridge read Bartram,
     probably in 1797-1798. Cites other passages from Travels
     to illustrate the "similar imagery and phraseology" and
     also "suggestive coincidence of moral feeling or sentiment"
     in Coleridge's work, especially "Kubla Khan." The "im-
     pression" Bartram left on Coleridge "was deep and lasting."
     Parallel passages from "Ruth" and Travels show Bartram's
     influence upon Wordsworth.

3   JACKSON, M. KATHERINE. "Outlines of the Literary History of
     Colonial Pennsylvania," Columbia University Studies in
     English and Comparative Literature, XIII, 145-8.
        William Bartram shows the influence of Rousseau and in
     turn influenced Wordsworth and Coleridge. His description
     of the Southeast shows the "simplicity of life...intense
     love of nature...rapt emotion" characteristic of him.

4   MORRIS, GEORGE S. "William Bartram," Cassinia: Proceedings
     of the Delaware Valley Ornithological Club, no. 10 (Febru-
     ary), 1-9.
        Biography of William Bartram (youth, travels in Florida).
     Travels (which sometimes resembles Defoe's work) is "rich
     in interest and graphic in its literary style." Bartram
     has a claim to "special recognition as an ornithologist."
     He did more work on American birds than any writer before
     Wilson; Wilson probably would not have completed his work
     without Bartram's encouragement and help.

1913 A BOOKS - NONE

1913 B SHORTER WRITINGS

1   [STICKLEY, GUSTAV.] "A Picturesque Old House in Philadelphia
     Recalling the Adventurous Lives of John and William Bar-
     tram, Early American Botanists," The Craftsman, XXIV (May),
     193-97.
        Brief description of the Bartram house in Philadelphia
     (built in 1731). More attention is actually given to an
     account of William Bartram's travels through "the savage
     wastes" of the South to discover American flora and fauna
     in Travels.

2   STONE, WITMER. "Bird Migration Records of William Bartram,
     1802-1822," Auk: A Quarterly Journal of Ornithology, XXX
     (July), 325-58.

1915

    (STONE, WITMER)
       William Bartram's manuscript "Calendar of Natural His-
tory, Memorable Events &c" is a daily record of observations on the weather, flora, and fauna, which covers (in-
completely) the years from 1802 to 1822. Stone has systematically arranged all of the references to birds, and
reproduces most of the record for January 1802, plus the
significant zoological data for 1802. Bartram's "Calendar"
is "a mine of information." The data on bird migration
constitute "the oldest record, covering a series of years,
that we have for any part of North America."

1915 A BOOKS - NONE

1915 B SHORTER WRITINGS

1   COOPER, LANE. "A Glance at Wordsworth's Reading," in Methods
and Aims in the Study of Literature. Boston: Ginn and
Co., pp. 110-24.
      Discusses Wordsworth's interest in travel literature,
including William Bartram's Travels, which Wordsworth probably knew "almost by heart." "Ruth" in places follows
Bartram "word for word." The Prelude and other Wordsworth
poems also show Bartram's influence.

1917 A BOOKS - NONE

1917 B SHORTER WRITINGS

1   BARNHART, JOHN H. Journal of the New York Botanical Garden,
XVIII (December), n. 239-40.
      Footnote on William Bartram's life. He had "the advan-
tage of a better education" than his father, and "of association with his father's scientific work from childhood."
He traveled south in 1772. "He was a botanical artist of
much enthusiasm and considerable ability."

2   COOPER, LANE. "Travellers and Observers, 1763-1846," in The
Cambridge History of American Literature, edited by William
P. Trent et al. Vol. I. New York: G. P. Putnam's Sons.
Reprinted. New York: The Macmillan Co., 1946, pp. 195-98.
      Summarizes the four parts of Travels. Selected quota-
tions (on nature and the Indians) illustrate "the richness
of form and color" in Bartram's work. Bartram's description of "a motion and a spirit in the environment" reveals
his "Neoplatonic and Hartleian philosophy."

1918 A BOOKS - NONE

1918 B SHORTER WRITINGS

1   CHINARD, GILBERT. L'Exotisme Américain dans l'Oeuvre de
        Chateaubriand. Paris: Hachette, pp. 246-72.
            Uses parallel passages to show Chateaubriand's extensive
        borrowings from William Bartram's Travels. Chateaubriand
        used Bartram's accounts of the flora, the fauna, and the
        Indians of Florida. In particular, he turned almost ex-
        clusively to Bartram for the landscape of Florida. Some-
        times the French author follows Bartram's words very
        closely and at other times the influence is more indirect.
        Chateaubriand usually adds "color" to Bartram's precise
        botanical descriptions.

2   GEE, WILSON. "William Bartram," Bulletin of the University
        of South Carolina, no. 72 (September), 17-19.
            Brief biography of William Bartram. Travels reports on
        his search for "rare and useful productions of nature" in
        the Southeast. "His treatment of the plants is not sys-
        tematic; but he mentions numbers of them in his description
        of the country, giving them their correct scientific names."
        The illustrations Bartram did for B. S. Barton's Elements
        of Botany showed "for the first time by illustration many
        of the most curious and beautiful plants of North America."
        Includes a bibliography of William Bartram's published
        works.

1919 A BOOKS - NONE

1919 B SHORTER WRITINGS

1   CHINARD, GILBERT. "Chateaubriand, Les Natchez, Livres I et
        II: Contribution à l'Étude des Sources de Chateaubriand,"
        University of California Publications in Modern Philology,
        VII (23 January), 205-6.
            Lists Travels among the American sources (along with
        works by Carver and Imlay) Chateaubriand used for Natchez.
        Bédier (WB.1903.B1) accused Chateaubriand of having added
        certain details to Bartram's descriptions. These details,
        absent in the French edition, are in the original English.
        Chateaubriand, therefore, did not have the French transla-
        tion at his disposal.

2   FOX, RICHARD HINGSTON. Dr. John Fothergill and His Friends:
        Chapters in Eighteenth Century Life. London: Macmillan
        and Co., pp. 185-91.

1921

(FOX, RICHARD HINGSTON)
   Collinson sought patrons who gave William Bartram com-
missions for drawings. Dr. Fothergill helped Bartram with
money for his journey through the southern colonies. Quotations illustrate the style of Travels. Bartram believed
the Indian was interested in white civilization and religion, hence he advocated an exchange program between the
two nations.

1921 A BOOKS - NONE

1921 B SHORTER WRITINGS

1   BARNHART, JOHN H. Journal of the New York Botanical Garden,
       XXII (July), n. 124-25.
          A footnote on William Bartram's life. "He had the ad-
       vantage of a better education than his father, and was an
       artist of considerable ability."

2   MacFARLANE, JOHN M. "The Evolution of Garden Flowers and
       Fruits in the Past Century," University Lectures Delivered
       by Members of the Faculty in the Free Public Lecture Course
       1919-1920: The University of Pennsylvania, VII, 263-85.
          Tells the story of a dream in which Botanicus and William
       Bartram take four excursions "amid Philadelphia environs."
       William Bartram observes the plants and fruits of 1920 and
       makes a few comments on the inventions of modern civiliza-
       tion and man's unchanging desire for warfare.

3   OWEN, THOMAS M. "Bartram, William," in History of Alabama
       and Dictionary of Alabama Biography. Vol. III. Chicago:
       The S. J. Clarke Publishing Co., pp. 109-110.
          A short paragraph. Biographical data on William Bartram,
       and description of his itinerary through the Alabama area.

1924 A BOOKS - NONE

1924 B SHORTER WRITINGS

1   HICKS, PHILLIP M. "II: The Beginnings of the Natural History
       Essay," in "The Development of the Natural History Essay in
       American Literature." Ph.D. dissertation, University of
       Pennsylvania, pp. 21-29.
          Travels is similar in form to the kind of journal kept
       by contemporary travelers, but the book shows two important
       differences. William Bartram's attitude toward nature, and

(HICKS, PHILLIP M.)
the "quality" of his observations. William Bartram's "Introduction" is the earliest natural history essay published in America. This "Introduction" introduces four elements into the literature of natural history: "scientific observation, aesthetic appreciation of nature, the belief in the immanence of the creative principle in nature, and the feeling of compassion for the suffering of the lower orders."

1925 A BOOKS - NONE

1925 B SHORTER WRITINGS

1   BISSELL, BENJAMIN. "The American Indian in English Literature of the Eighteenth Century," YSE, LXVIII, 21-22, 46-47, 77.
        William Bartram was one of the romantic writers who used the Indian to ridicule civilization and to praise natural goodness. Many writers of the period attacked the institutions of society by pointing out how well the Indians got along with only the guidance of nature. Bartram's Utopia is peopled by Indians "living in all the perfection of primitive simplicity."

1927 A BOOKS - NONE

1927 B SHORTER WRITINGS

1   EXELL, A. W. "William Bartram and the Genus Asimina in North America," The Journal of Botany, British and Foreign, LXV (March), 65-70.
        Errors in the labeling of drawings in Travels have led to confusion on two species (Annona pigmaea, Annona incarna), described and collected by William Bartram.

2   LOWES, JOHN LIVINGSTON. The Road to Xanadu. New York: Houghton Mifflin, pp. 7-11, 186-88, 364-70, 452-55, 506, 513-16, 586-89.
        Studies the influence of Travels on the imagery of Coleridge and Wordsworth. Coleridge's Notebook contains quotations from Travels (alligators, exotic plants, birds, tropical thunderstorms, fountains). Demonstrates in detail the similarity between specific passages from Bartram and the imagery in "The Ancient Mariner" and "Kubla Khan." Bartram also influenced "Fears in Solitude" and perhaps "Lewti." Wordsworth's "She was a phantom of delight" shows

1928

    (LOWES, JOHN LIVINGSTON)
      Bartram's influence and "Ruth" is "saturated with Bartram."
      A passage from Dorothy Wordsworth's Journals has parallels
      with Bartram. Travels is "subliminated" in Lafcadio
      Hearn.

1928 A BOOKS - NONE

1928 B SHORTER WRITINGS

1   [ANDERSON, EDGAR SHANNON.] "American Botanical Gardens and
        English Poetry," Missouri Botanical Garden Bulletin, XVI
        (November), 115-22.
          Travels "had a tremendous vogue and rightly so." Even
      the scientific descriptions are "imaginative and stimu-
      lating." The descriptions of southeastern Indians are
      still the best first-hand account for that time. Quotes
      Lane Cooper on William Bartram's influence on Wordsworth.
      Shows parallel passages from Travels and the "Prelude" and
      "Ruth." Quotes Lowes' analysis of Coleridge's notebook to
      demonstrate the influence of William Bartram on Coleridge.

2   ANON. "Notes of a Rapid Reader," SatR, IV (21 April), 775.
          Wordsworth and especially Coleridge (as Lowes points out)
      drew from the "lush descriptions" in William Bartram's
      Travels. William Bartram loved all animals except the
      alligator and pictured the Indian as a noble savage. "This
      is what the New World was like to a loving spirit, thrilled
      by nature, and conscious of beauty."

3   ANON. "The Bartrams: The Travels of William Bartram," SatR,
        IV (21 April), 786.
          Introduces the American Bookshelf reprint of Travels
      (which has "long been out of print"). Gives biographies
      of John and William Bartram. Travels should appeal to
      botanists, students of ethnology, and lovers of literature.
      The Bartrams influenced the English Romantic movement and
      belong to that movement. They contributed to English
      thought the image of the Indian as happy, noble savage.

4   ANON. "The Travels of William Bartram," The Nation, CXXVI
        (21 March), 326, 328.
          Expresses surprise that Travels has been forgotten. It
      is a "narrative of infinite riches and variety." Bartram
      is "by turns enthusiastic, sober, dramatic, idyllic; re-
      flective, naive; diffusive, firm; redundant, precise."

5   VAN DOREN, MARK. "Editor's Note," in Travels of William Bartram, edited by Mark Van Doren. New York: Dover Publications, Inc., pp. 5-6.

      Discusses Bartram's influence on Wordsworth and Coleridge and quotes Carlyle's praise of Travels. Bartram's book is "valuable not only for its poetry and narrative but for its botanical and ethnological record."

6   WHERRY, EDGAR T. "The History of the Franklin Tree, Franklinia Alatamaha," Journal of the Washington Academy of Sciences, XVIII (19 March), 172-76.

      The "Franklin tree" (Franklinia alatamaha Marshall) was first discovered by John Bartram in 1765. William Bartram described his second view of the tree (1773) in Travels and named it after Franklin. Another sighting was recorded in 1790. Since this date, the plant has never been found growing wild. Wherry theorizes that later searchers misjudged the location and that the original plants were destroyed by fire. The species survived because nurserymen took cuttings from the tree Bartram transplanted to his garden.

1929 A BOOKS - NONE

1929 B SHORTER WRITINGS

1   C[OOPER], L[ANE]. "William Bartram," in Dictionary of American Biography, edited by Allen Johnson. Vol. I. New York: Charles Scribner's Sons, pp. 28-29.

      Summarizes William Bartram's life, travels, and writings. Besides the famous and influential Travels, Bartram produced a number of shorter pieces (particularly on birds and plants), a diary, a manuscript pharmacopoeia, and drawings. Bartram also gave much information as well as encouragement to other scientists.

2   EXELL, A. W. "Two Eighteenth-Century American Naturalists: John and William Bartram," Natural History Magazine, II, 50-58.

      Briefly discusses the journal, collection of dried plants, and paintings and drawings Bartram sent Dr. Fothergill, which are now housed in the British Museum. Reproduces several drawings. "Bartram was an artist of no mean ability," but "as a scientist he had perhaps too strong a tendency towards the picturesque; for his desire to produce an elegant and balanced picture made him disregard to a rather alarming extent the relative proportions of the components of his pictures." See also (JB1929.B2).

1930

3   H., F. "Browsing through Bartram," The Christian Science Moni-
        tor, XXI (2 May), 11.
            At times there is a "poetry" in William Bartram's "simple
        prose" that equals Coleridge's lyricism. Discusses speci-
        fic images and descriptions from Travels that influenced
        Coleridge's "Rime of the Ancient Mariner," "Kubla Khan,"
        "Lewti," and Wordsworth's "Ruth."

1930 A BOOKS - NONE

1930 B SHORTER WRITINGS

1   HARPER, FRANCIS. "Alligators of the Okefinokee," Scientific
        Monthly, XXXI (July), 51-67.
            William Bartram's description of alligators was doubted
        by later commentators, but only a few details need to be
        verified. "The fidelity and accuracy of Bartram's account
        as a whole, with only the slightest indulgence in poetic
        license, are most impressive." William Bartram gives the
        "only genuine first-hand account by a naturalist" of the
        bellowing of the alligator.

1931 A BOOKS - NONE

1931 B SHORTER WRITINGS

1   BARNHART, JOHN H. "Bartram Bibliography," Bartonia, Special
        issue, supplement to no. 12 (31 December), 51-67.
            Lists, with occasional brief annotation: published
        writings of John Bartram (books, papers); publications re-
        lating to John and William Bartram and the Bartram Garden;
        catalogs of the Bartram Garden. Extensive list of minor
        secondary sources.

2   CHESTON, MRS. EDWARD M. "Permanent Bartram Exhibition at the
        Academy of Natural Sciences," Bartonia, Special issue, sup-
        plement to no. 12 (31 December), 68.
            Lists and describes some of the books and personal pos-
        sessions belonging to John and William Bartram that compose
        a permanent exhibit at the Academy of Natural Sciences.

3   FAGIN, N. BRYLLION. "Bartram's Travels," MLN, XLVI (May),
        288-91.
            The London (1792 and 1794) and Dublin (1793) editions of
        William Bartram's Travels modified the original Philadelphia

(FAGIN, N. BRYLLION)
edition (1791). The English editors objected to Bartram's
"exuberance of style." "They recast phrases, improved his
punctuation, and occasionally reworded a passage. The re-
sult is a more or less tame Bartram, the Philadelphia nature enthusiast repressed and 'corrected.'" Examines and
illustrates the types of changes made in the text. The
German edition (1793), translated by E. A. W. Zimmermann,
shows "a definitely modified Bartram."

4   SMALL, JOHN K. "Bartram's _Ixia Coelestina_ Rediscovered,"
Journal _of_ _the_ _New_ _York_ _Botanical_ _Garden_, XXXII (July),
155-61.
The "botanical rediscovery" of Bartram's _Ixia coelestina_
in the flat woods north of Gainesville, Florida. The
flowers were "so numerous that Bartram's statement about
'azure fields of cerulian Ixea' seems perfectly justifi-
able." Quotes William Bartram on the plant, describes and
provides a sketch of it, and discusses the history of its
discovery.

5   STONE, WITMER. "The Work of William, Son of John Bartram,"
Bartonia, Special issue, supplement to no. 12 (31 December),
20-23.
Bartram was a zoologist as well as a botanist. _Travels_
is "a landmark in the progress of American ornithology."
Bartram also deserves credit for encouraging other zoolo-
gists (Thomas Say, B. S. Barton, Alexander Wilson).

1933 A   BOOKS

1   FAGIN, N. BRYLLION. _William_ _Bartram_: _Interpreter_ _of_ _the_
American _Landscape_. Baltimore: Johns Hopkins Press.
Part I covers Bartram's life, character, philosophy of
nature, and Indian studies. He prefers the primitive to
the civilized, but his romantic idealization of the Indian
is combined with careful scientific observation. Part II
discusses Bartram's landscape and his art. He observes as
scientist, poet and philosopher, describes nature with the
eyes of a painter. His diction is sometimes simple, sometimes "florid." Part III investigates Bartram's literary
influence, especially on Coleridge and Wordsworth, but also
other English and American writers (Lamb, Shelley, Carlyle,
Emerson, Thoreau, Chivers, Hearn), and Chateaubriand. Com-
prehensive bibliography stresses literary interest in
Bartram.

1936

1933 B SHORTER WRITINGS

1   JENKINS, CHARLES F. "The Historical Background of Franklin's
        Tree," PMHB, LVII (July), 193–208.
            In 1765 John and William Bartram discovered and named the
        "Franklin tree" (Franklinia alatamaha). Article includes
        William's watercolor of the tree and a map of the location
        in Georgia. William again encountered the grove of trees
        in 1773, and brought back plants or seeds to Pennsylvania.
        Since 1790, no one has seen the plant growing wild; hence,
        every Franklinia can be traced back to the one in the
        Bartram garden.

1936 A BOOKS – NONE

1936 B SHORTER WRITINGS

1   HARPER, FRANCIS. "The Vultur Sacra of William Bartram," Auk,
        n.s. LIII (October), 381–92.
            The bird William Bartram described under the name of
        "Vultur sacra" ("Painted Vulture") has not been accounted
        for satisfactorily until now. Ornithologists (in particu-
        lar J. A. Allen) have doubted its existence. Bartram's
        description of the "Vultur sacra" applies very satisfac-
        torily to Sarcoramphus papa (L.), the King Vulture. A
        discrepancy in the color of the tail may have been caused
        by Bartram's misinterpreting some information he received
        from the Indians. Bartram's manuscript reports to Dr.
        Fothergill include a description of "The Croped Vulture"
        which aids in identifying the bird.

1937 A BOOKS – NONE

1937 B SHORTER WRITINGS

1   HARPER, FRANCIS, and ARTHUR N. LEEDS. "A Supplementary Chap-
        ter on Franklinia Alatamaha," Bartonia, no. 19 (8 March),
        1–13.
            The Franklin tree (Franklinia alatamaha Marshall) was
        discovered in 1765 in Georgia by John and William Bartram,
        and has never been discovered growing wild after 1790.
        William Bartram reports on a spring flowering season, but
        the flowering season apparently varies according to lati-
        tude. Discusses evidence for locating the exact locality
        of the species and its ecological distribution. Describes
        "the long search" for Franklinia. Lists illustrations of

(HARPER, FRANCIS...)
Franklinia and discusses possible causes of extinction of the wild specimens.

1938 A   BOOKS - NONE

1938 B   SHORTER WRITINGS

1   CHESTON, EMILY R. "William Bartram," in John Bartram, 1699-
    1777; His Garden and His House; William Bartram, 1739-1823.
    Philadelphia: John Bartram Association, pp. 16-21.
       Biography of William Bartram. Describes highlights of
    his trip through the South. The influence of Travels on
    Coleridge and Wordsworth. The book has "extraordinary
    merits" and is an "authoritative" record of the Indians
    and of flora and fauna. The drawings for B. S. Barton's
    Elements of Botany are the only extant drawings by William
    Bartram in this country.

1939 A   BOOKS - NONE

1939 B   SHORTER WRITINGS

1   BRANNON, PETER A. "Through the Years: The Route of William
    Bartram," in The Montgomery Advertiser (25 June).
       Francis Harper is in Alabama to map the routes Bartram
    took through Alabama while traveling for Dr. Fothergill in
    1777 and 1778. Describes the area as depicted in Bartram's
    journal, and makes comparisons with contemporary conditions.
    Bartram shipped his plants through British merchants at
    Pensacola and Mobile.

2   FAGIN, N. BRYLLION. "William Bartram, 'Prophet Without
    Honor,'" New York Times Book Review (5 February), p. 2.
       Travels went almost unnoticed in America, but in Europe
    it was much admired and highly influential, especially
    among the English Romantic poets. Bartram was neither a
    trained writer nor a trained scientist. His composition
    was "gentle, undirected; his style was lush and discursive."

3   HARPER, FRANCIS. "The Bartram Trail through the Southeastern
    States," Bulletin of the Garden Club of America, 7th ser.,
    no. 5 (September), 54-64.
       Harper retraced the Bartram routes from Philadelphia
    through Virginia, the Carolinas, Georgia, Alabama, and
    Florida. He compares some of the scenes, buildings, roads,

1940

(HARPER, FRANCIS)
plants and animals he encountered with the descriptions
supplied by the Bartrams. Bartram enthusiasts aided the
task of retracing the routes. The discovery of a 1772 map
followed by William Bartram has resolved questions about
the route across Georgia and Alabama. "Perhaps the climax
of the whole trip was the identification of the very lagoon
where the younger Bartram had his terrific adventures with
the alligators, and of the near-by shell mound where he
camped!"

4   ____. "William Bartram's Centennial," Scientific Monthly,
XLVIII (April), 380-84.
Lists and describes commemorative exercises, exhibits,
publications, and celebrations during the 200th anniversary
of William Bartram's birth. Travels is a "literary treas-
ure and ... a contribution of the first rank to American
natural history and ethnology of the eighteenth century."
Bartram's veracity as a naturalist has been pretty well
vindicated. He is "our most commanding figure in zoology
... between Mark Catesby and Alexander Wilson." The task
of fully identifying many plants and some animals he describes is still unfinished.

5   PYLE, FRANCIS C. "William Bartram's Voyage," Subtropical
Gardening (December), pp. 12-14.
Follows part of Bartram's journey up the St. Johns River
in Florida. Includes maps of the route. The description
in Travels of this expedition reveals Bartram's "passionate
quest" for new species, capacity for losing his own identity
when observing flora and fauna, versatile gifts, "unfailing,
gentle manner."

1940 A BOOKS

1   EARNEST, ERNEST. John and William Bartram: Botanists and
Explorers. Philadelphia: University of Pennsylvania Press.
William Bartram's life, from youth through old age. The
itinerary and significant events of Travels. Bartram's
theory of nature ("alive," "conscious," and "unified," the
probable source of Wordsworth's "religion of nature").
Bartram's ideas represent the "spirit of the century"; he
accepted both the classical faith in reason and the romantic belief in emotion and intuition, and also stressed the
need for balancing the two. His picture of the Southeastern
Indians is "one of the best we have for the period." Poetry
and science were "sister muses" in the eighteenth century;
the work of the Bartrams shows this lost unity.

1940 B   SHORTER WRITINGS

1   HARPER, FRANCIS. "Some Works of Bartram, Daudin, Latreille,
       and Sonnini, and Their Bearing upon North American Herpe-
       tological Nomenclature," American Midland Naturalist,
       XXIII (May), 692-723.
          "Bartram was the most notable of the eighteenth-century
       commentators on North American amphibians and reptiles, and
       his account of the American alligator is an immortal classic
       on that species." F. M. Daudin used Bartram's Travels in
       describing new species. Discusses specific species as
       described by Bartram and Daudin.

2   LOWES, JOHN LIVINGSTON. "Introduction," in The Travels of
       William Bartram, edited by Mark Van Doren. New York:
       Barnes and Noble, pp. 5-6.
          Bartram's Travels "lives again" in Dorothy Wordsworth's
       Journal. Her brother's "Lewti" and "Ruth" are "steeped in
       Bartram." Travels also helped Coleridge write "Dejection,"
       "Kubla Khan" (also "steeped in Bartram") and many entries
       of his Memorandum Book. Displays parallel passages from
       these works and Travels.

1942 A   BOOKS - NONE

1942 B   SHORTER WRITINGS

1   HARPER, FRANCIS. "Two More Available Plant Names of William
       Bartram," Bartonia, no. 21 (27 May), 6-8.
          John and William Bartram discovered the shrub currently
       known as Pinckneya pubens (the Georgia bark). In the same
       manuscript notes William Bartram proposes the name
       bracteata, which has priority and should replace Michaux's
       pubens. William Bartram's manuscript notes also prove that
       Franklinia alatamaha and Pinckneya were seen close to-
       gether. William Bartram must also supersede Pursh as the
       author of the name of Magnolia pyramidata.

2   _____. "William Bartram's Names of Birds," Proceedings of the
       Rochester Academy of Science, 4th ser. VIII, 208-21.
          Summarizes the debate between Coues and Allen on the use
       of Bartram's names for birds. Harper agrees with Coues'
       defense of Bartram. The American Ornithologists' Union
       Check-list progressively eliminated Bartram's names. Harper
       discusses specific bird names from Travels, in order "to
       select those of Bartram's names that are binomial, are ac-
       companied by nomenclaturally valid descriptions, are iden-
       tifiable beyond reasonable question, and have priority."

1943

1943 A   BOOKS - NONE

1943 B   SHORTER WRITINGS

1   HARPER, FRANCIS. "Quercus Incana Bartram," Bartonia, no. 22
         (7 May), 3.
             Lack of an adequate index to Travels has prevented recog-
         nition of all the available plant names in it. Bartram's
         name Quercus incana, applied to the upland willow oak, has
         priority and must replace Michaux's (Q. cinera Michx.).

2   SCUDDER, HAROLD H. "Bartram's 'Travels': A Note on the Use
         of Bartram's 'Travels' by the Author of 'Nick of the
         Woods,'" N&Q CLXXXIV (13 March), 154-55.
             "American authors as well as the English read Bartram."
         When describing one of his chief characters in the second
         chapter of Nick of the Woods, Robert Montgomery Bird alludes
         to the passage in which William Bartram describes an "old
         champion" among the alligators.

1944 A   BOOKS - NONE

1944 B   SHORTER WRITINGS

1   HARPER, FRANCIS. "Introduction," in Travels in Georgia and
         Florida, 1773-74: A Report to Dr. John Fothergill, by
         William Bartram, edited by Francis Harper. Transactions
         of the American Philosophical Society, n.s. XXXIII (Novem-
         ber), 123-33.
             A Report to Dr. Fothergill is useful when compared with
         Travels. It supplies additional information on Bartram's
         itinerary and method of composition, and contains "beauti-
         ful descriptive passages similar to those in the Travels."
         Discusses recent field investigations on the Bartram
         routes. Quotes from the many commentators who have doubted
         Bartram's accuracy and defends Bartram's "fundamental in-
         tegrity." "The imperfections in his work are minor ones
         that do not seriously impair the magnificent monument to
         American natural history that he has erected." Discusses
         editorial policy with regard to the Report.

2   _____. "Literature Cited," in Travels in Georgia and Florida,
         1773-74; A Report to Dr. John Fothergill, by William
         Bartram, edited by Francis Harper. Transactions of the
         American Philosophical Society, n.s. XXXIII (November),
         228-31.
             Bibliography of editions and reprints of John and William
         Bartram's works, secondary sources on William, and sources

1946

(HARPER, FRANCIS)
that provide information to clarify or supplement William
Bartram's writings.

3   RICKETT, HAROLD W. "Legitimacy of Names in Bartram's
     'Travels,'" Rhodora: The New England Botanical Club, XLVI
     (November), 389-91.
        Travels "does not meet current requirements for the pub-
     lication of specific epithets," because Bartram did not
     consistently employ the Linnean system of binary nomencla-
     ture for species. Bartram used binomials "pretty consis-
     tently in listing species which he had seen; occasionally,
     however, lapsing into polynomials...." Gives examples of
     Bartram's names.

1945 A BOOKS - NONE

1945 B SHORTER WRITINGS

1   MERRILL, E. D. "In Defense of the Validity of William Bar-
     tram's Binomials," Bartonia, no. 23 (23 November), 10-35.
        William Bartram uses about 358 binomials as compared with
     only two entries without binomials. Hence Bartram's work
     cannot be eliminated on the basis of the International
     Rules. Includes a list of Bartram's new species with their
     original descriptions, and a supplementary list of his
     nomina nuda. The number of new Bartram binomials is about
     130.

1946 A BOOKS - NONE

1946 B SHORTER WRITINGS

1   HARPER, FRANCIS. "Proposals for Publishing Bartram's Travels,"
     The American Philosophical Society Library Bulletin, 1945,
     pp. 27-38.
        Reprints a broadside in which Enoch Story, Jr., proposes
     publishing Travels by subscription (probably in 1786). If
     the book had been published at this date, Bartram would
     have received more credit than he has for naming new spe-
     cies. Quotes from letters by B. S. Barton to William Bar-
     tram, on Barton's (apparently unsuccessful) plans for pub-
     lication of Travels. Prints the proposal to publish
     Travels made by the Philadelphia printers James and Johnson,
     who published the book sometime in 1791.

1949

<u>1949 A   BOOKS - NONE</u>

<u>1949 B   SHORTER WRITINGS</u>

1   TOLLES, FREDERICK B.   "Writers of the Middle Colonies," in
         <u>Literary</u> <u>History</u> <u>of</u> <u>the</u> <u>United</u> <u>States</u>, edited by Robert E.
         Spiller, et al. Vol. I. New York: Macmillan Co., pp. 92-93.
           <u>Travels</u> is "an authentic literary masterpiece of early
         American romanticism." Bartram had "an artist's eye and a
         richly varied verbal palette." His style, "the most dis-
         tinctive and accomplished style developed by any writer in
         the middle colonies," is "loose in structure, fluent in
         movement ... equally apt for detailed delineation and for
         rapid narrative." His reports on Indians were anthropo-
         logically sound. His pantheism mixes his Quaker background
         with deism.

<u>1951 A   BOOKS - NONE</u>

<u>1951 B   SHORTER WRITINGS</u>

1   MURDOCK, KENNETH B.   "Woolman, Crèvecoeur, and the Romantic
         Vision of America," in <u>The</u> <u>Literature</u> <u>of</u> <u>the</u> <u>American</u>
         <u>People</u>, <u>an</u> <u>Historical</u> <u>and</u> <u>Critical</u> <u>Survey</u>, edited by Arthur
         H. Quinn. New York: Appleton-Century-Crofts, pp. 134-35.
           William Bartram "had a painter's eye for form and color."
         His best work shows "simplicity and freshness." Bartram
         used his large vocabulary "with scientific precision but
         also with care for aesthetic values." "From the literary
         point of view no earlier account of American travel ex-
         celled it."

<u>1953 A   BOOKS - NONE</u>

<u>1953 B   SHORTER WRITINGS</u>

1   HARPER, FRANCIS.   "William Bartram and the American Revolu-
         tion," <u>PAPS</u>, XCVII (30 October), 571-77.
           William Bartram repeatedly praised peace and never men-
         tioned the Revolutionary War in <u>Travels</u>. Nevertheless,
         there is some evidence that he supported the cause of the
         Revolution and may have taken part in it in a minor way.
         George Ord, Bartram's first biographer, wrote that Bartram
         joined a detachment of men in 1776 to repel an erroneously
         reported invasion of Florida. Other evidence for Bartram's
         support of the war is circumstantial: the "Quaker

(HARPER, FRANCIS)
unorthodoxy" in Bartram's family; his admiration for
leaders of the Revolution; his pride in American independence.

1954 A BOOKS - NONE

1954 B SHORTER WRITINGS

1   HERBST, JOSEPHINE. New Green World. New York: Hastings
        House.
            William Bartram becomes prominent in chapters 8-14 of
        this biography of John Bartram. The early chapters treat
        William Bartram's failure to successfully establish himself
        in an occupation. Chapter 11 uses John Bartram's journal
        to present the trip to Florida taken by father and son to-
        gether. Chapter 14 is devoted to William alone, largely
        to Travels, in which he retraces the earlier trip to
        Florida. Stresses the "joy" in William Bartram's vision:
        "Everything that he witnesses is acceptable."

2   LEARY, LEWIS. "Bartram, William," in Articles on American
        Literature, 1900-1950. Durham, N.C.: Duke University
        Press, p. 18.
            Lists journal articles on William Bartram from 1900-1950.

1955 A BOOKS - NONE

1955 B SHORTER WRITINGS

1   GUMMERE, RICHARD M. "William Bartram, A Classical Scientist,"
        Classical Journal, L (January), 167-70.
            Both style and content of Travels reflect the Greco-Roman
        tradition. Bartram's Indians are reminiscent of Greeks
        and Romans. His vision of nature is closer to the Panthe-
        ism of the Stoics than to Deism or Neo-Platonism. Displays
        Bartram's allusions to classical myth and the classical
        vocabulary he uses to describe Florida. Bartram's ornate
        style is "a continuous bouquet of what the ancient gram-
        marians called the 'Asianic' or free style rather than the
        simple and condensed Attic."

1956

1956 B   SHORTER WRITINGS

1   BELL, MALCOLM, JR.   "Eye Witnesses to a Vanished America,"
         GaR, X (Spring), 13-23.
             Quotes William Bartram on the beauties of the little town
         of Sunbury in Georgia. He contributed more than his father
         to our knowledge of early southeastern America. Travels
         became a source book on Indian lore and influenced Words-
         worth, Coleridge and other noted writers. See also
         (JB1956.B1).

2   WRIGHT, JOHN K.   "From 'Kubla Khan' to Florida," AQ, VIII
         (Spring), 76-80.
             Travels has been explored separately by lovers of poetry
         and lovers of nature. It has been "next to impossible" to
         identify the exact localities Bartram visited until publi-
         cation of Harper's annotated edition of Travels and A Re-
         port to Dr. John Fothergill (WB1944.B1). The three springs
         described by Bartram which influenced "Kubla Khan" are
         identified by Harper, but the "Isle of Palms" cannot be
         located.

1957 A   BOOKS - NONE

1957 B   SHORTER WRITINGS

1   BRADFORD, ROBERT W.   "A Poetic Botanist," in "Journey into
         Nature: American Nature Writing, 1733-1860." Ph.D. dis-
         sertation, Syracuse University, pp. 114-59.
             Travels has "a curious pictorial quality, a power of
         landscape delineation." Biography. General philosophical
         ideas reflected in Travels include piety, sympathy for ani-
         mals, interest in Indians, primitivism. Examines the aes-
         thetic principles of the Bartram landscape: Bartram was
         indebted to eighteenth-century ideas of the sublime and the
         picturesque.

2   CADBURY, B. BARTRAM.   "Foreword," in John and William Bartram's
         America: Selections from the Writings of the Philadelphia
         Naturalists, edited by Helen Gere Cruickshank. New York:
         Devin-Adair Company, pp. v-vi.
             John and William Bartram were important in the develop-
         ment of American science. John Bartram's scant writing is
         "rather labored." William Bartram took over the task of
         reporting on their work and did so with realism and humor.

(CADBURY B. BARTRAM)
William's work has never been as well known in America as
in other countries. The Bartrams were "intrepid travellers" who faced many dangers.

3   CRUICKSHANK, HELEN GERE. "Introduction," in John and William
Bartram's America: Selections from the Writings of the
Philadelphia Naturalists, edited by Helen Gere Cruickshank.
New York: The Devin-Adair Company, pp. xi-xix.
The Bartrams saw the American wilderness "with the eyes
of great botanists, of philosophers, explorers, historians,
and ecologists." John Bartram's journals were "blunt and
brief as a captain's log." William Bartram's entries were
"vivid and joyous." John Bartram's personality was more
forceful; William Bartram had "a poet's appreciation" for
nature. Travels furnishes "the first genuinely artistic"
picture of the Southeast.

1958 A   BOOKS - NONE

1958 B   SHORTER WRITINGS

1   EDELSTEIN, J. M. "America's First Native Botanists," The
Library of Congress Quarterly Journal of Current Acquisitions, XV (February), 51-59.
Discusses the complete collection of early editions of
major works by John and William Bartram now owned by the
Library of Congress. Summarizes their lives, gives background on their travels, and describes and quotes their
works. John Bartram's Observations is an "exciting and
highly readable book ... one of the most charming early
travel narratives by an American." In Travels, William
Bartram redescribed much that his father had written of
in his Journal; the description of fountains that influenced Coleridge uses language similar to John Bartram's.

2   HARPER, FRANCIS. "Introduction," in The Travels of William
Bartram, Naturalist's Edition, edited by Francis Harper.
New Haven: Yale University Press, pp. xvii-xxxv.
Sketches William Bartram's early life. Travels relates
the "climactic experiences" of his life, "indelible im-
pressions of his contacts with both wild and human nature."
Discusses the preparation and publication of the book. The
stimulation of John Bartram's household and the example of
other botanists who kept journals were important influences
on Travels. William Bartram did not receive credit for
naming certain species of plants and animals because of the

1963

(HARPER, FRANCIS)
delay in publishing his book. Travels met with a "generally indifferent reception." The book was neglected in America, but there were many editions in Europe. Provides brief histories for fourteen of the naturalists with whom Bartram developed friendships in his later years.

3   ____. "Preface," in The Travels of William Bartram, Naturalist's Edition, edited by Francis Harper. New Haven: Yale University Press, pp. v-xii.
The "naturalist's edition" was undertaken to supply the following information on Bartram's Travels: current names of plants and animals and their distribution; routes; Indian traders and trading posts; names and locations of streams and mountains; incidental items in the colonial life of the Southeast; Indian village sites, tribal movements, characteristics. Discusses efforts to retrace the Bartram routes. "Over literally hundreds of miles the present-day follower of Bartram need not deviate more than a few feet ..."

4   ____. "References: Literature (Including Manuscripts)," in The Travels of William Bartram: Naturalist's Edition, edited by Francis Harper. New Haven: Yale University Press, pp. 668-89.
Bibliography of primary sources on John and William Bartram (editions, reprints, translations, manuscripts), secondary sources on them (especially on their scientific achievements), works useful in clarifying and supplementing their writings.

1963 A BOOKS

1   SUTTON, ANN, and MYRON SUTTON. Exploring with the Bartrams. Eau Claire, Wis.: E. M. S. Hale Company.
Biography of John and William Bartram for children. Based on the Bartrams' own writings. Emphasizes their exploration of the American wilderness. Illustrations include maps, photographs, and drawings by William Bartram.

1963 B SHORTER WRITINGS - NONE

1967 A BOOKS - NONE

1967 B SHORTER WRITINGS

1   FOX, FRANK. "The Eden World of William Bartram," in Phi Alpha
     Theta Student. Salt Lake City: University of Utah,
     pp. 12-23.
         Travels presents an Eden, "a sensual and colorful gar-
     den" in which innocence predominates. The landscape is
     generally dark and shadowed, while strong light focuses
     attention on objects of interest. Bartram recognized the
     justice and necessity of violence and death in "the
     jungle." Bartram's Eden is most serene during the evening;
     his Indian is "an unfallen Adam-like figure ..."

2   MATTFIELD, MARY S. "Journey to the Wilderness: Two Travelers
     in Florida, 1696-1774," Florida Historical Quarterly,
     XXXXV (April), 327-51.
         Two Quaker travel narratives describe the Florida coast:
     Jonathan Dickinson's God's Protecting Providence (1696),
     and William Bartram's Travels (1791). Each is "typical" of
     travel literature and also "transcends" the genre to become
     true literature. As characteristic travelers, both men
     show energy, courage, acute observation, and curiosity.
     For both "the wilderness journey" becomes a metaphor.
     William Bartram's journey is a "spiritual pilgrimage in
     which nature plays the unifying role" Dickinson assigned
     to Divine Providence.

1968 A BOOKS - NONE

1968 B SHORTER WRITINGS

1   CORNER, GEORGE W. "Foreword," in William Bartram: Botanical
     and Zoological Drawings, 1756-1788, edited by Joseph Ewan.
     Philadelphia: American Philosophical Society, pp. vii-viii.
         William Bartram's drawings for Dr. Fothergill (owned by
     the British Museum) are for the first time reproduced "in
     a manner fully adequate to reveal their excellence." The
     album of drawings is a work of art and a scientific docu-
     ment. "Some of the drawings present the first report of a
     species new to science ... others give valuable information
     on the distribution of various animals and plants."

2   EWAN, JOSEPH. "Bibliographic References," in William Bartram:
     Botanical and Zoological Drawings, 1756-1788, edited by
     Joseph Ewan. Philadelphia: American Philosophical Society,
     pp. 168-72.

1969

(EWAN, JOSEPH)
Bibliography of manuscripts and published works by John
and William Bartram, secondary sources (including manuscripts) supplying information on them, and general information on topics related to their work, particularly in
science and ethnology.

3   _____. "Introduction," in William Bartram: Botanical and
Zoological Drawings, 1756-1788, edited by Joseph Ewan.
Philadelphia: American Philosophical Society, pp. 3-43.
Examines William Bartram's work as naturalist and artist;
his plant discoveries and descriptions; the contribution of
the Bartram Garden to horticulture; Bartram's work with
birds, reptiles, fish, mammals, insects, shells, and the
American Indian; the history and present whereabouts of
Bartram's drawings. Presents a full chronology of his
life. Bartram is "the one indigenous colonial artist of
merit for natural history." Among the drawings for Dr.
Fothergill, twenty-three species were firsts, a record un-
matched by other explorers. Lists the six catalogs on the
Bartram Garden, "an overlooked fund of information on horticulture in the U.S."

1969 A BOOKS

1   SULLIVAN, WILLIAM J. "Towards Romanticism: A Study of
William Bartram." Ph.D. dissertation, University of Utah.
William Bartram was "one of America's pioneer Romantics."
Chapter I: John Bartram as a rational, secular-minded
exemplar of the Enlightenment. Chapter II: William Bartram's "return to nature" as a protest against the urban
and secular world of Philadelphia. Chapter III: William
Bartram viewed nature as a living and spiritual organism
and saw man's "reason" as "akin to intuition." Chapter
IV: William Bartram's retreat to the wilderness for joys
of primitive life. Chapter V: Indians (romantic noble
savages, but also "real" Indians based on direct observation). Chapter VI ("The Travels as Romantic Literature"):
Nature is symbolic of the lost Eden; the narrator shows
other elements of "a true Romantic hero" (subjectivity,
harmony with nature, adventure and exploration).

1969 B SHORTER WRITINGS

1   BUSCH, FRIEDER. "William Bartrams Bewegter Stil." In Litera-
tur und Sprache der Vereinigten Staaten: Aufsätze zu Ehren
Hans Galinsky, edited by Hans Helmcke; Klaus Lubbers; and

1972

(BUSCH, FRIEDER)
Renate Schmidt–v. Bardeleben. Heidelberg, Germany: Carl
Winter Universitätsverlag, pp. 47–61.
William Bartram's description constantly presents movement. The movement is a matter of style and unifies form
and content. Analyzes a passage from Bartram's <u>Report to
Dr. Fothergill</u>, 1776, demonstrating the variety of movement
attained through prepositions (which alternately show movement and stasis) and through frequent use of participles.
Bartram's originality consists in his dynamic, self-over-
flowing landscape. Analyzes a passage from <u>Travels</u> which
shows Bartram's characteristic movement and counter-
movement.

2   DAVIS, RICHARD B. "William Bartram (1793–1823)," in <u>American
Literature</u> through <u>Bryant</u>, <u>1585–1830</u>. New York: Appleton-
Century-Crofts, pp. 107–108.
Short list of selected primary and secondary sources.

1970 A BOOKS - NONE

1970 B SHORTER WRITINGS

1   LEARY, LEWIS. "Bartram, William," in <u>Articles</u> on <u>American
Literature</u>, <u>1950–1967</u>. Durham, N.C.: Duke University
Press, p. 25.
Lists journal articles on William Bartram from 1950–1967.

1972 A BOOKS - NONE

1972 B SHORTER WRITINGS

1   LEE, BERTA G. "William Bartram: Naturalist or 'Poet'?" <u>EAL</u>,
VII (Fall), 124–29.
The famous description of alligators in <u>Travels</u> has been
the subject of much controversy. Summarizes previous commentators who defended or attacked Bartram's accuracy.
Demonstrates that some details of his description belong
"only to poetry." Analyzes the same scene in the earlier
<u>Report</u> to <u>Dr</u>. <u>Fothergill</u> to prove Bartram "used all the
tools of fiction to provide interesting and readable adventures" in <u>Travels</u>.

2   MEDEIROS, PATRICIA M. "Chapter II: William Bartram," in
"The Literature of Travel of Eighteenth-Century America."
Ph.D. dissertation, University of Massachusetts, pp. 16–49.

1973

(MEDEIROS, PATRICIA M.)
Bartram's "rhythmic pattern" alternates description, narration, and adventure. The "tension" between subjective and objective perception gives the book "its special point of view." The style shows Bartram's scientific and artistic motives. The self-effacing persona does not present full characterization of people except Indians. Bartram's themes include the abundance of natural goods, man's waste of nature, the link between progress and destruction, the interrelation of man and nature.

1973 A BOOKS - NONE

1973 B SHORTER WRITINGS

1   DeWOLF, GORDON. "Introduction," in Travels through North and South Carolina, Georgia, East and West Florida, by William Bartram. Savannah, Ga.: The Beehive Press, pp. v-xx.
        Describes horticultural activity in Philadelphia and in the Carolinas, Georgia, and Florida during Bartram's age. Bartram seldom reported to Dr. Fothergill; hence Travels is a "scientific disappointment." "Perhaps Bartram should be considered as an artist who grew up in an atmosphere of natural history, rather than as a horticultural collector who could draw."

1974 A BOOKS - NONE

1974 B SHORTER WRITINGS

1   SPILLER, ROBERT E., et al., eds. "John and William Bartram," in Literary History of the United States: Bibliography. 4th ed., rev. New York: Macmillan Co., pp. 398-99, 874-75, 1147-48.
        Lists separate works, collected works, primary sources, bibliography, selected biographical and critical works.

Writings About William Byrd II, 1817 - 1974

1817 A BOOKS - NONE

1817 B SHORTER WRITINGS

1   PAULDING, JAMES KIRKE. Letters from the South, Written during
         an Excursion in the Summer of 1816. Vol. I. New York:
         J. Eastburn & Co., pp. 27-29.
           Paulding read Byrd's manuscripts ("with wonderful gusto")
         while visiting Virginia. He summarizes the Indian de-
         scription of heaven in the History. The History is "the
         finest specimen of that grave, stately, and quaint mode of
         writing fashionable about a century ago, that I have ever
         met with anywhere."

1839 A BOOKS - NONE

1839 B SHORTER WRITINGS

1   RUFFIN, EDMUND. "The Last Communications of George E. Har-
         rison, of Brandon," The Farmer's Register, VII (28 Febru-
         ary), 106-8.
           Prints a letter from George E. Harrison discussing the
         "Byrd manuscript." Harrison has allowed the Virginia His-
         torical Society to copy it. He also grants Ruffin per-
         mission to publish it in The Farmer's Register with "such
         alterations and corrections . . . as the form of the
         author may require."

1841 A BOOKS - NONE

1841 B SHORTER WRITINGS

1   RUFFIN, EDMUND. "Editor's Preface," The Farmer's Register,
         Appendix to Vol. IX, iii-iv.
           Describes the Byrd manuscript volume ("the only copy in
         existence") containing the "Westover Manuscripts" published

1843

    (RUFFIN, EDMUND)
        in The Farmer's Register. The manuscripts were not written
        to be published. Byrd's "great freedom of expression, and
        of censure" add to their interest, but probably prevented
        earlier publication. "Col. Byrd was a true and worthy in-
        heritor of the opinions and feelings of the old cavaliers
        of Virginia." Published separately as The Westover Manu-
        scripts (B1841.B2).

2   _____. "Editor's Preface," in The Westover Manuscripts, Con-
        taining the History of the Dividing Line Betwixt Virginia
        and North Carolina; A Journey to the Land of Eden, AD.
        1733; and a Progress to the Mines. Written from 1728 to
        1736 and Now First Published. Petersburg, Va.: Edmund and
        Julian C. Ruffin, pp. iii-iv. Also published in The Far-
        mer's Register (B1841.B1).

3   _____. "Publication of the Byrd Manuscripts," The Farmer's
        Register, IX (31 October), 577.
        "There has been no publication previously made of these
        curious and interesting writings, and neither is there in
        existence any copy of the time-worn original manuscripts,
        which were placed at our disposition by the owner, the late
        George E. Harrison of Brandon." Believes the work will be
        as "acceptable" to readers as it is "valuable to the
        literary public."

1843 A BOOKS - NONE

1843 B SHORTER WRITINGS

1   SIMMS, WILLIAM GILMORE. "Ruffins' Publications," Magnolia,
        n.s. II (April), 259-60.
        Review of Ruffin's edition of the "Westover Manuscripts."
        Praises Byrd's History and quotes it extensively. Byrd has
        a talent for selecting the significant, avoiding the un-
        necessary, and informing without tiring the reader. The
        History abounds in "the singular fact, the lively picture,
        the interesting tradition, the adroit or witty expression."

1851 A BOOKS - NONE

1851 B SHORTER WRITINGS

1   ANON. "Colonel William Byrd," Virginia Historical Register
        and Literary Note Book, IV (April), 75-77.

(ANON.)
Provides an account of Byrd's life and character. The
"Westover Manuscripts," published by Ruffin, are "well
worth reading for the curious and amusing information which
they contain relating to the natural and social history of
our State, and for the clear and pleasing style in which
they are written."

2   CAMPBELL, CHARLES. "The Westover Library," Virginia Historical Register and Literary Note Book, IV (April), 87-90.
Campbell introduces Lyman C. Draper's description of the
"catalogue of the Westover library," detailing the number
and kinds of books. Draper also lists names of several men,
including himself, who purchased books that had belonged to
the library.

1855 A   BOOKS - NONE

1855 B   SHORTER WRITINGS

1   DUYCKINCK, EVERT A., and GEORGE L. DUYCKINCK. "William Byrd,"
in Cyclopaedia of American Literature. Vol. I. New York:
Charles Scribner. Reprinted. Detroit: Gale Research
Company, 1965, pp. 79-82.
Quotes the summary of Byrd's life given on his tombstone.
The History shows "sharp outline in description and fresh-
ness of feeling in sentiment." The humor comes from "a
good natural vein" and an acquaintance with both books and
society. Byrd was "in intimacy with what was best in the
old world and the new." Parts of the History are "worthy"
of Fielding. Byrd's satire is similar to Irving's. Byrd
narrates the journey "in a clear, straightforward manner,"
shows "ready wit," and is "a vivid describer of a wild
beast or an Indian."

1866 A   BOOKS - NONE

1866 B   SHORTER WRITINGS

1   WYNNE, THOMAS H. "Introduction," in History of the Dividing
Line and Other Notes, from the Papers of William Byrd of
Westover in Virginia, Esquire, edited by Thomas H. Wynne.
Vol. I. Richmond, Va.: Printed for private circulation,
pp. ix-xix.
Biography of Byrd. Quotes epitaph on his tomb. His
"most enduring Monument" is in his writings. Quotes
Ruffin's "Preface" from the "Westover Manuscripts."

1871

> (WYNNE, THOMAS H.)
> Includes a note from a Byrd descendant giving further his-
> tory of the manuscripts. Wynne's edition reprints the ori-
> ginal manuscript, following its "accidental and chaotic Ar-
> rangement" to approximate a facsimile. The edition includes
> "numerous Expressions...which, probably because they were
> thought too free" were altered or suppressed in the 1841
> edition. Describes Byrd's "Parchment-bound Folio."

1871 A BOOKS - NONE

1871 B SHORTER WRITINGS

1   CHAPIN, J. R. "The Westover Estate," Harper's Magazine, XLII
       (May), 801-10.
         Describes a trip to Westover in 1869. Includes a de-
       scription of the site and layout of the house, its important
       rooms, and the grounds. Records the inscriptions on the
       tombstones. Gives an account of the lives of Byrd and his
       father, the legends of Evelyn Byrd, the history of Westover
       under William Byrd III and during the Revolution. Byrd
       "shed abroad over the circle of his influence a halo which
       has lasted"; his travel narratives are "important papers."

1878 A BOOKS - NONE

1878 B SHORTER WRITINGS

1   TYLER, MOSES COIT. "Literature in the South: IV," in History
       of American Literature, 1607-1765. New York: G. P. Putnam's
       Sons. Reprinted. New York: The Crowell-Collier Publishing
       Company, pp. 486-93.
         Tyler selects from the History ("one of the most delight-
       ful of the [colonial] literary legacies") representative
       passages to show Byrd's characteristic style: his "gayety,"
       his humor and sarcasm, his skillful depiction of nature,
       the Indian, and the inhabitants of Lubberland.

1891 A BOOKS - NONE

1891 B SHORTER WRITINGS

1   HARRISON, CONSTANCE C. "Colonel William Byrd of Westover,
       Virginia," Century Illustrated Monthly Magazine, XLII
       (June), 163-78.

(HARRISON, CONSTANCE C.)
Describes Westover as a visitor experienced it in 1891.
Includes several drawings of interior and exterior of the
house. Reproductions of the portraits of Byrd, his family,
and his friends, accompanied by biographical sketches. Re-
counts romantic legends of the Byrd family, e.g., tales of
Evelyn Byrd's abortive romance and role as Westover's
resident ghost.

1892 A BOOKS

1   HARLAND, MARION [TERHUNE, MARY HAWES]. His Great Self.
       Philadelphia: J. B. Lippincott Company.
       A novel based on legends that Byrd refused to let his
       daughter Evelyn marry the Earl of Peterborough. Evelyn's
       lover comes to America, is kidnapped and shipped out of the
       country by Byrd; Evelyn dies (after forgiving her father).
       Byrd is presented as "the masterful lord of the manor,"
       highly admirable except in his rash behavior toward his
       daughter. Presents a romanticized image of plantation
       life at Westover.

1892 B SHORTER WRITINGS - NONE

1901 A BOOKS - NONE

1901 B SHORTER WRITINGS

1   ANON. "Letters of William Byrd, 2d, of Westover, Va.," VMHB,
       IX (October), 113-30.
       Short introduction on Byrd's life and descendants. The
       letters are reprinted from copies at Brandon, the Harrison
       family seat, where most of Byrd's letters are found.

2   BASSETT, JOHN SPENCER. "Introduction," in The Writings of
       Colonel William Byrd, of Westover in Virginia, Esquire,
       edited by John Bassett. New York: Doubleday,
       pp. ix-xxxviii.
       A sketch of the Byrd family which supplied much informa-
       tion to later biographers. Contains the first extensive
       account of William Byrd II's life. Most of the information
       came from manuscripts, including personal letters. Focuses
       on the "industrial [economic], social, and political posi-
       tions" of Byrd and his father. An especially detailed his-
       tory of Byrd's political quarrels and advocacies. Brief
       notice of Byrd's "sprightly" and "genial" literary produc-
       tions.

1902

1902 A BOOKS - NONE

1902 B SHORTER WRITINGS

1   ANON. "The Writings of 'Colonel William Byrd of Westover in
       Virginia Esq'r.'" VMHB, IX (April), 445-47.
          Review of Bassett's edition. Byrd's "vigorous" style
       shows "careless ease and quaint humor." He shows "an un-
       failing zest in life, and a power to make a companion of
       his reader." Objects to the inclusion of "two very gross
       letters."

2   EARLE, ALICE MORSE. "A Virginia Gentleman of Two Centuries
       Ago," The Dial, XXXII (1 May), 308-10.
          Review of Bassett's edition. Byrd's writings have great
       value as literature and history. Byrd equals Franklin's
       "forceful, lucid and charming English." His best work
       provides a "very candid" portrait of the man himself.

1904 A BOOKS - NONE

1904 B SHORTER WRITINGS

1   ANON. "Notes and Queries: The Byrd Library at Westover,"
       VMHB, XII (October), 205-7.
          Quotes an advertisement for the catalog of the Byrd
       library printed in the Virginia Gazette (1777). Describes
       the manuscript of the catalog preserved in Philadelphia:
       physical characteristics, order in which books are arranged,
       title page.

2   HOLLADAY, ALEXANDER Q. "Social Conditions in Colonial North
       Carolina," The North Carolina Booklet, III (February),
       5-30.
          Counters the criticism of North Carolina presented in the
       History. There were churches in North Carolina, so Byrd
       was wrong in charging neglect of religion. The influential
       men of the community, the refined homes, the cultured so-
       ciety disprove the charges of idleness and "grossness of
       living."

William Byrd II: A Reference Guide

1910 A BOOKS - NONE

1910 B SHORTER WRITINGS

1   WERTENBAKER, THOMAS J. Patrician and Plebeian in Virginia.
        Charlottesville, Va.: Published by the author. Reprinted.
        New York: Russell & Russell, 1959, pp. 137-41.
          The Byrd family provides the best example of the develop-
        ment of the colonial Virginia gentleman. William Byrd I
        was a merchant prince. William Byrd II combined business
        instincts with the manners and habits of the cavalier.
        William Byrd III lacked business acumen but maintained the
        cavalier mannerisms. All were distinguished in the poli-
        tical life of the colony and were esteemed by their con-
        temporaries. All had a sense of public obligation.

1916 A BOOKS - NONE

1916 B SHORTER WRITINGS

1   ANON. "Notable Southern Families, The Byrd Family," The Look-
        out, VIII (30 December). n.p.
          Genealogy of the Byrd family, from William Byrd I through
        descendants living in 1916. Describes the Byrd coat of
        arms. Concludes with the story of "the fair Evelyn," who
        died when her love for the grandson of the Earl of Peter-
        borough was forbidden by her father.

1917 A BOOKS - NONE

1917 B SHORTER WRITINGS

1   WINSHIP, GEORGE P. "Travellers and Explorers, 1583-1763," in
        The Cambridge History of American Literature, edited by
        William P. Trent, et al. Vol. I. New York: G. P. Putnam's
        Sons. Reprinted. New York: Macmillan Co., 1946, pp. 10-11.
          Byrd's travel journals have "permanent value." Quota-
        tions illustrate Byrd's humor. Byrd's writings prove the
        learning and literary culture of the educated colonial.

1922 A BOOKS - NONE

1922 B SHORTER WRITINGS

1   SWEM, EARL G. "Introductory Note," in Description of the
        Dismal Swamp and a Proposal to Drain the Swamp, by William

1924

    (SWEM, EARL C.)
       Byrd of Westover, edited by Earl G. Swem. Metuchen, New
      Jersey: C. F. Heartman, pp. 7-13.
       This previously unpublished proposal was written between
      1728 and 1737. Byrd later abandoned the project. Describes
      later efforts to drain the swamp.

1924 A BOOKS - NONE

1924 B SHORTER WRITINGS

1   ANON. "Virginia Council Journals, 1726-1753, (Vol. 605-1418),"
        VMHB, XXXII (January), 22-37.
         Factual sketch of Byrd's busy life and financial affairs.
        Describes the house and grounds at Westover; lists Byrd's
        descendants. Reprints Byrd's letters to Charles Boyle,
        the Earl of Orrey, and his son. The letters reveal Byrd's
        relationships with English friends and knowledge of English
        affairs. Includes several photographs of Byrd's grave and
        the house and gates at Westover.

1927 A BOOKS - NONE

1927 B SHORTER WRITINGS

1   ANON. "Letters of the Byrd Family," VMHB, XXXV (July), 221-45.
         General introduction to a series of articles reprinting
        letters of the Byrd family (from William Byrd I through
        the generation of William Byrd III). Focuses on William
        Byrd I and gives a detailed genealogy of the Byrd family.
        The letters (including those of William Byrd II) were taken
        from a manuscript compiled by a Byrd descendant; the ori-
        ginals were "apparently lost" by 1927.

2   ANON. "Letters of the Byrd Family," VMHB, XXXV (October),
        371-89.
         Outlines the main events of Byrd's life as a prelude to
        printing his letters and business documents. Discusses the
        history of Kneller's portrait of Byrd and requests funds to
        have it copied for the Virginia Historical Society.

3   HAZARD, LUCY LOCKWOOD. "Colonel William Byrd of Westover in
        Virginia, Esquire," in The Frontier in American Literature.
        New York: Frederick Ungar Publishing Co., Inc., pp. 55-62.
         Byrd is the most brilliant example of the "cavalier aris-
        tocracy" of the Southern frontier. Contrasts Byrd's

(HAZARD, LUCY LOCKWOOD)
freedom from "race prejudice," his "Catholic" (sacramental and formalistic) religion, his "poetical" interest in "what is curious or lovely in the world" with the Puritans' prejudice against inferior races, their Protestantism, and "preoccupation with the things of the next world."

4   PARRINGTON, VERNON LOUIS. "The Frontier: Lubberland," in Main Currents in American Thought, The Colonial Mind. New York: Harcourt, Brace and Company. Reprinted. New York: Harcourt, Brace and World, Inc., 1954, pp. 141-42.
      Byrd's "chatty narrative" is the "earliest detailed description of the fringe of squatter settlements." His account of Lubberland reveals the distrust of government and the "social laissez faire" which became important components of American democracy.

1928 A BOOKS - NONE

1928 B SHORTER WRITINGS

1   VAN DOREN, MARK. "Editor's Note," in A Journey to the Land of Eden and Other Papers by William Byrd. New York: Macy-Masius, pp. 5-6.
      Byrd was "the most interesting Virginian of his time, and one of the most interesting of all colonial writers." Sketches his biography and introduces the three travel narratives. Byrd was "a keen and humorous observer of human beings; and a writer of remarkable charm, clarity, and strength." His works are important for the fidelity with which he depicts frontier Virginia.

1929 A BOOKS - NONE

1929 B SHORTER WRITINGS

1   BOYD, WILLIAM K. "Introduction," in William Byrd's Histories of the Dividing Line Betwixt Virginia and North Carolina, by William Byrd. Raleigh: The North Carolina Historical Commission, pp. xi-xxvii.
      The accuracy of the History must be reexamined because the Secret History differs significantly. The Secret History provides more information on the men Byrd quarreled with; additional incidents such as violence to frontier women; a number of letters, addresses and documents not in the History. The History contains more information on the

1930

(BOYD, WILLIAM K.)
region, and Byrd's criticism of the people of North Carolina. Supplies a history of the boundary controversy and
of the expedition. Brief introduction to Byrd's life and
character.
Reprinted (B1967.B1).

2   BRUCE, PHILIP ALEXANDER. "Colonel William Byrd," in The Virginia Plutarch. Vol. I. Chapel Hill: University of
North Carolina Press, pp. 135-54.
Traces Byrd's family background and his life in England
and Virginia. Presents a highly favorable estimate of his
character: "In the whole history of the community [co-
lonial Virginia] there is not to be discovered a man of
more varied accomplishments, more polished deportment, more
winning temper...." Franklin alone surpassed Byrd as a
colonial writer. The latter's letters and travel narratives exhibit his graceful style, acute knowledge of his
world, and appealing personality.

1930 A BOOKS - NONE

1930 B SHORTER WRITINGS

1   W[ERTENBAKER], T[HOMAS] J. "William Byrd," in Dictionary of
American Biography, edited by Allen Johnson. Vol. III.
New York: Charles Scribner's Sons, pp. 383-84.
Outlines the main events of Byrd's life, stressing his
public career, in particular, his quarrel with Governor
Spotswood. His travel journals and letters "show a grace,
wit, and sprightliness unique among the colonists." Byrd
himself exhibits the "grace, charm, the culture but also
the rather lax business methods of the Virginians of the
eighteenth century."

1932 A BOOKS

1   BEATTY, RICHMOND CROOM. William Byrd of Westover. Boston:
Houghton Mifflin Company.
Full-length biography. Presents a highly favorable portrait of Byrd's character, but shows the "reality" behind
the myth of the Virginia Cavalier by stressing aspects of
life such as debts and money problems. Provides information on the English background (particularly the literary
climate) and emphasizes Byrd's constant desire to return
to England when living in America. Gives details on

1934

(BEATTY, RICHMOND CROOM)
Virginia society, politics and economics. Written before
the discovery of the diaries, uses Byrd's letters and public documents as chief sources of information, and is inaccurate with reference to Byrd's private life. Summarizes
the three travel narratives. As a writer, Byrd was "primarily a humorist." Includes a bibliography of sources on
Byrd and his age.
Reprinted 1970.

1932 B   SHORTER WRITINGS

1   WOODFIN, MAUDE H.   "William Byrd and the Royal Society," VMHB,
        XL (January, April), 23-34, 111-23.
           Describes Byrd's participation in the Royal Society while
        living in England and America. He presented gifts, in-
        cluding a live rattlesnake, and showed special interest in
        the botany, zoology and mineralogy of Virginia.

1934 A   BOOKS - NONE

1934 B   SHORTER WRITINGS

1   HOULETTE, WILLIAM D.   "The Byrd Library," Tyler's Quarterly
        Historical and Genealogical Magazine, XVI (October),
        100-109.
           Byrd purchased most of the books for the Byrd library.
        Describes types of books, with sample titles, using the
        catalog of the library in Bassett's edition of Byrd's works.
        Culls references to his reading from Byrd's own writings.

2   _____.   "William Byrd and Some of His American Descendants,"
        Tyler's Quarterly Historical and Genealogical Magazine, XVI
        (October), 93-100.
           Brief biographies of William Byrd I, William Byrd II, and
        the men of the succeeding four generations who achieved
        prominence in American history.

3   LYLE, GUY R.   "William Byrd, Book Collector," American Book
        Collector, V (May-June, July), 163-65, 208-11.
           Byrd's library shows great diversity in subject matter,
        and also a high proportion of foreign languages. It repre-
        sents the cultural level of many upper class Virginians.
        The duplication of titles in the library probably indicates
        the extent to which borrowing from private collections was
        common.

1935

1935 A BOOKS - NONE

1935 B SHORTER WRITINGS

1   MURDOCK, KENNETH B. "William Byrd and the Virginian Author
          of The Wanderer," Harvard Studies and Notes in Philology
          and Literature, XVII, 129-36.
            John Fox dedicated Mottos of the Wanderer (1718), quota-
          tions from Fox's ephemeral English literary periodical,
          The Wanderer, to Byrd. Byrd replied with a letter (written
          on the fly-leaf of a copy of the book) in which he repudi-
          ates the liberty taken in putting his name "on the Title-
          page of no extraordinary Performance" and mocks the ful-
          someness of the praise offered to him. Byrd says that he
          sends Fox a guinea not out of gratitude but as a "bribe to
          do it no more."

2   PATTEE, FRED L. The First Century of American Literature:
          1770-1870. New York: D. Appleton-Century Co., pp. 248-50.
            Byrd was "admirably balanced and accomplished." The fact
          he never tried to publish the History ("a graphic bit of
          realism") proves Southerners had little interest in pub-
          lishing anything that was not "practical." "Here was an
          accomplished author, who in England undoubtedly would have
          been able to stand with the literary masters, writing a
          classic and seeking no publisher."

1937 A BOOKS - NONE

1937 B SHORTER WRITINGS

1   KRAUS, MICHAEL. "William Byrd," in A History of American His-
          tory. New York: Farrar and Rinehart, pp. 74-77.
            Sketches Byrd's life. Compares the History with the
          Secret History. The former is "a fairly faithful picture
          of the frontier," but the "tart" comments on North Caro-
          lina, taken as authentic by later historians, are mislead-
          ing. Byrd "was fond of the frontier, but he was not so
          careful a student of the psychology of the frontiersman as
          was Crèvecoeur."

2   MASTERSON, JAMES R. "William Byrd in Lubberland," AL, IX
          (May), 153-170.
            Collects Byrd's strictures upon North Carolina (Lubber-
          land) under the following six categories: disadvantages
          due to geography, climate favoring laziness, neglect of re-
          ligion, lack of government control, attractiveness to

(MASTERSON, JAMES R.)
outcasts, and the desire of those on the border to be on the Carolina side. Marshalls an impressive body of evidence from other travelers to support Byrd's charges.

3 MONAHAN, KATHERINE. "William Byrd of Westover, Explorer of Early America," Scholastic, XXXI (18 December), 21-23.
Biography. Byrd "had all the intellectual curiosity of a true scholar" and was a true cavalier. Few people know the "Westover Manuscripts." Byrd's accounts of his journeys are "delightful, overflowing with keen wit, the joyousness of living, and shrewd observations on manners, customs, and people." Explains the background of the History; discusses and quotes Byrd's comments on the Carolinians, Indians, and nature.

1938 A BOOKS - NONE

1938 B SHORTER WRITINGS

1 CANNON, CARL L. "William Byrd II of Westover," The Colophon, n.s. III (Spring), 291-302.
Detailed description of the Byrd library, based on the catalog printed in Bassett's edition of Byrd (B1901.B2). Analyzes the library as a key to Byrd's interests and tastes. The library was sold to Isaac Zane (not, as reported, at auction in Philadelphia). The books are widely scattered; few have been located. Enumerates libraries containing books with the Byrd bookplate.
Reprinted in American Book Collectors and Collecting from Colonial Times to the Present (B1941.B1).

1939 A BOOKS - NONE

1939 B SHORTER WRITINGS

1 ANON. "Evidence Relating to Westover," VMHB, XLVII (July), 191-217.
Article reprints documents from the Byrd "Title Books," composed primarily of wills and deeds which detail the growth of the Westover estate from 1637 to 1744.

2 McILWAINE, SHIELDS. "William Byrd of Westover Discovers the Frontier Lubber," in The Southern Poor-White from Lubberland to Tobacco Road. Norman: Oklahoma University Press, pp. 3-15.

1940

(McILWAINE, SHIELDS)
The History furnishes "the first vivid picture of the
poor whites." Byrd's lack of sympathy for this class is
explained by his status as an aristocrat and by the con-
tempt generally felt by Virginians toward North Carolinians.
Using the lubbers as a target for his wit, Byrd stressed
their laziness. "Nevertheless, his brilliant group-por-
trait of the lubbers was accurate and is still largely
true on the lowest level."

3   WRIGHT, LOUIS B. "A Shorthand Diary of William Byrd of Westover," The Huntington Library Quarterly, II (July), 489-96.
A manuscript diary, in shorthand, covering 1709-1712,
was recently discovered at the Huntington Library and de-
ciphered. The diary is a significant source of information on the planters of colonial Virginia (manners, politics, economic conditions), on Byrd himself (his diet,
reading, religion). Prints sample passages from the de-
ciphered journal and also prints two pages showing Byrd's
shorthand notations. Other portions of the diary have been
located at the University of North Carolina and the Virginia Historical Society.

4   _____. "The Classical Tradition in Colonial Virginia," PBSA,
XXXIII, 85-97.
Byrd's almost daily reading in Greek (along with frequent reading in Latin and Hebrew) shows his "serious and
scholarly attitude toward the classics" and exemplifies the
"tradition of Renaissance learning" in eighteenth-century
America. Other planters also cultivated the classics.
Surveys libraries of Virginia to demonstrate the high per-
centage of classical works and works in the classical
languages. Byrd owned "most of the works of Greek and
Roman writers then available."

1940 A   BOOKS - NONE

1940 B   SHORTER WRITINGS

1   BEATTY, RICHMOND CROOM, and WILLIAM J. MULLOY. "Introduction,"
in William Byrd's Natural History of Virginia; or, The
Newly Discovered Eden, edited and translated by Richmond
Croom Beatty and William J. Mulloy. Richmond: The Dietz
Press, pp. v-xxviii.
Introduces first translation and republication of Neu-
gefundenes Eden (1737). The book includes the "most de-
tailed account in existence of the natural history of

(BEATTY, RICHMOND CROOM...)
colonial Virginia," and much information on the geographical, social, and political structures of the colony in the
1730s. The book was apparently written by Samuel Jenner.
Beatty and Mulloy supply evidence (in particular, Byrd's
efforts to attract Swiss settlers to his land) to prove
that Byrd furnished the information on Virginia.

2   RIBACK, WILLIAM H. "Some Words in Byrd's Histories," American
Speech, XV (October), 331-32.
In the History and the Secret History, Byrd uses the
words quixot, chicane, virtuoso, spongy or spungy, and
isinglass. Some are usually attributed to a later date,
and some are used for perhaps the first time in American
writings.

3   WRIGHT, LOUIS B. "The Byrds' Progress from Trade to Genteel
Elegance," in The First Gentlemen of Virginia. San Marino,
California: The Huntington Library, pp. 312-48.
Tells the story of William Byrd I's rise to wealth and
power and William Byrd II's more brilliant social, economic, political and cultural life. This cycle is typical
of many later American families. Includes an introduction
to Byrd's writings. William Byrd II "lived in greater
elegance and with more fitting grace than any of his contemporaries" and was "the herald of the eighteenth-century
order of Virginia gentlemen."

4   WRIGHT, LOUIS B., and MARION TINLING. "William Byrd of Westover, an American Pepys," SAQ, XXXIX (July), 259-74.
Byrd received the epithet "The American Pepys" because
of the History, but the discovery of the diary makes that
name far more appropriate. The comparison with Pepys is
justified. Both "mention all manner of trifling things";
both recount troubles with their wives. Byrd's diary reveals his character and his times. We learn about his
reading, wife and servants, social life, religion, and
diet.
Reprints a series of excerpts from the 1709-1712 diary.

1941 A BOOKS - NONE

1941 B SHORTER WRITINGS

1   CANNON, CARL L. "William Byrd II of Westover," in American
Book Collectors and Collecting from Colonial Times to the
Present. New York: H. W. Wilson Company, pp. 13-26.

1942

    (CANNON, CARL L.)
        Reprinted from <u>The Colophon</u> (B1938.B1).

2   WRIGHT, LOUIS B. "Introduction," in <u>The Secret Diary of</u>
       <u>William Byrd of Westover</u>, <u>1709-1712</u>, edited by Louis B.
       Wright and Marion Tinling. Richmond: The Dietz Press,
       pp. v-xxv.
        Byrd's diary (the "earliest extensive diary in the
       South") reveals his personal habits, attitudes and beliefs,
       and broad range of interests and activities. "The most
       significant revelations . . . recreate the daily life on
       a great plantation." Byrd gives an accurate picture of
       the cavalier planter instead of the distorted myth.

1942 A BOOKS - NONE

1942 B SHORTER WRITINGS

1   WILSON, JAMES SOUTHALL. "William Byrd and His Secret Diary,"
       <u>WMQ</u>, 2d ser. XXII (April), 165-74.
        The 1709-1712 diary substitutes fact for the "glamorous"
       Byrd of history and legend. "A hard-headed, strong-willed
       man of affairs," Byrd was "a typical man of his time,--so
       much above the average that he is the epitome as well as
       the apogee of his day and his class." The diary is most
       valuable for the picture of life in early Virginia.

2   WOODFIN, MAUDE H. "Introduction," in <u>Another Secret Diary of</u>
       <u>William Byrd of Westover</u>, <u>1739-1741</u>, edited by Maude H.
       Woodfin and Marion Tinling. Richmond: The Dietz Press,
       pp. xiii-xiv.
        Recounts Byrd's life using the yet unpublished 1717-1721
       diary, and features the excitement of the London years.
       Notes similarities between the 1739-1741 diary and the
       other extant sections. Discusses the letters and literary
       exercises published in this volume, briefly analyzing con-
       tent and style, and emphasizes Byrd's kinship with the
       writers of neoclassical London.

3   _____. "Preface," in <u>Another Secret Diary of William Byrd of</u>
       <u>Westover</u>, <u>1739-1741</u>, edited by Maude H. Woodfin and Marion
       Tinling. Richmond: The Dietz Press, pp. iii-ix.
        Describes the Byrd manuscripts discovered in 1936 at the
       University of North Carolina (the 1739-1741 diary and the
       letters and literary pieces published in this volume). The
       1709-1712 diary was discovered at the Huntington Library.
       and the 1717-1721 diary at the Virginia Historical Society.

(WOODFIN, MAUDE H.)
>Recounts the discovery of the type of shorthand Byrd used and the decoding of the manuscripts.

1944 A   BOOKS - NONE

1944 B   SHORTER WRITINGS

1   TYLER, DOROTHY. "Modern Education and William Byrd of West-over," SAQ, XLIII (April), 174-80.
>Byrd's diary shows that wealthy Virginians were commonly sent abroad for schooling, and continued at home such English educational practices as the use of tutors. In Byrd's day, humanistic education was accepted without question. References in the diary to Byrd's constant reading prove him "an American·pioneer in continuing and adult education."

2   WOODFIN, MAUDE H. "Thomas Jefferson and William Byrd's Manuscript Histories of the Dividing Line," WMQ, 3d ser. I (October), 363-73.
>In 1815 the American Philosophical Society asked Thomas Jefferson's aid in identifying the author of a manuscript (Byrd's original draft of the History). Jefferson proved Byrd was the author and supplied, from the "Westover Manuscripts," copies of missing pages. Jefferson also secured for the Society the hitherto unknown Byrd manuscript of the Secret History.

1945 A   BOOKS - NONE

1945 B   SHORTER WRITINGS

1   LONN, ELLA. The Colonial Agents of the Southern Colonies. Chapel Hill: University of North Carolina Press, pp. 118-23, 213, 273-74, 375.
>Discusses Byrd's service in representing the Virginia assembly in England. He acted as special agent five times during the years 1697-1720. "He represented the type of colonial who would be a logical choice for agent--a staid planter of established position, distinguished family, and wealth, a member of the council...a cultured gentleman, and in addition, a man of long experience in England with many important contacts."

2   WOODFIN, MAUDE H. "The Missing Pages of William Byrd's 'Se-
         cret History of the Line,'" WMQ, 3d ser. II (January),
         63-70.
              The manuscript of the Secret History was incomplete when
         Jefferson discovered it and sent it to the American Philo-
         sophical Society. Boyd's edition (1929) used the incom-
         plete manuscript. The missing pages (taken from a fragment
         of one of Byrd's early drafts) are reprinted in this
         article.

3   WRIGHT, LOUIS B. "Introduction," in An Essay upon the Govern-
         ment of the English Plantations on the Continent of America
         (1701): An Anonymous Virginian's Proposals for Liberty
         under the British Crown, with Two Memoranda by William
         Byrd, edited by Louis B. Wright. San Marino, Ca.: The
         Huntington Library, pp. ix-xxiv.
              William Byrd II is not the author of this essay (which
         may have been written by Robert Beverley or William Byrd I),
         but he may have revised it. Ideas similar to those in
         the essay are found in the notebook (written in William
         Byrd II's handwriting) from which the memoranda published
         with the essay were taken.

4   _____. "William Byrd I and the Slave Trade," HLQ, VIII
         (August), 387-97.
              William Byrd I was principal owner of at least one slave
         ship. Captured by a French privateer, the ship was sold
         in France. William Byrd II drew up a petition to the
         Board of Trade in protest of this act. The petition, re-
         printed here, denounces the seizure as a bad precedent and
         danger to English trade and appeals to the English preju-
         dice against the French as "a most encrouching People."

5   _____. "William Byrd's Defense of Sir Edmund Andros," WMQ,
         3d ser. II (January), 47-62.
              Byrd defended Governor Andros against the charges brought
         by Blair that Andros was thwarting the clergy and the Col-
         lege of William and Mary. The article prints for the first
         time a detailed defense from a notebook in Byrd's hand-
         writing and explains the reasons for the quarrel and the
         background for the defense.

6   _____. "William Byrd's Opposition to Governor Francis Nichol-
         son," The Journal of Southern History, XI (February),
         68-79.
              Byrd was appointed colonial agent to explain why the
         Virginia House of Burgesses opposed Nicholson's plans for

(WRIGHT, LOUIS B.)
aiding New York during the threat of war. A notebook in Byrd's handwriting contains arguments against Nicholson's efforts to split the post of auditor and receiver general (held by Byrd) and to prevent the planting of flax and cotton in the tobacco colonies. Byrd argued that the latter policy "would force colonials to become Adamites and go naked."

1947 A BOOKS - NONE

1947 B SHORTER WRITINGS

1   LEARY, LEWIS. "A William Byrd Poem," WMQ, 3d ser. IV (July), 356.
        A poem found among the papers of St. George Tucker is attributed to Byrd.

2   WEATHERS, W. T. "William Byrd: Satirist," WMQ, 3d ser. IV (January), 27-41.
        Byrd's early writings (1696-1726) show a thirty years' apprenticeship to the trade of writer as practiced by Augustan London and reveal a developing epigrammatic style. The results are apparent in his later American writings. A long practice in writing "characters" climaxed in the satirical portraits of the Secret History.

3   WRIGHT, LOUIS B. The Atlantic Frontier: Colonial American Civilization, 1607-1763. New York: Knopf, pp. 72, 92-93, 300.
        The planter society of the early eighteenth century was "zealous in the pursuit of intellectual and spiritual development." Byrd was an "ornamental" member of this society and his devoted methodical study would also have done credit to a professional scholar.

1949 A BOOKS - NONE

1949 B SHORTER WRITINGS

1   SIOUSSAT, ST. GEORGE. "The Philosophical Transactions of the Royal Society in the Libraries of William Byrd of Westover, Benjamin Franklin, and the American Philosophical Society," American Philosophical Society Library Bulletin, XCIII, 99-113.
        Byrd was the first native colonial American to be elected a Fellow of the Royal Society. Describes the

1951

(SIOUSSAT, ST. GEORGE)
catalog of the Byrd library, which lists the Philosophi-
cal Transactions of the Royal Society. After the death of
William Byrd III, the library was purchased by Isaac Zane,
Jr., who sold the books in Philadelphia. The American
Philosophical Society purchased the Transactions in 1801.

2   WRIGHT, LOUIS B. "The Colonies: Writers of the South," in
Literary History of the United States, edited by Robert E.
Spiller, et al. Vol. I. New York: Macmillan Co., pp. 45-46.
Byrd is the most widely known writer of the colonial
South, "a man of learning and a virtuoso in science." The
diary is "a significant and revealing document," which
shows his devotion to classical learning. Two of the
three known portions of the diary have been published.
Byrd's most important literary work is the History. His
three travel journals are "spirited narratives."

1951 A   BOOKS - NONE

1951 B   SHORTER WRITINGS

1   MURDOCK, KENNETH B. "Early Travellers and Observers," in
The Literature of the American People: An Historical and
Critical Survey, edited by Arthur H. Quinn. New York:
Appleton-Century-Crofts, pp. 32-34.
Brief introduction to Byrd's writings, with focus on
qualities of Byrd's style. Byrd's "easy wit" was often
aimed at the unsophisticated. Byrd's History ("representa-
tive of his manner and method") was revised for "literary
effect," as Murdock proves with examples. Byrd's local
pride in Virginia evinces "his rudimentary feeling for
America as America."

1952 A   BOOKS - NONE

1952 B   SHORTER WRITINGS

1   WATKINS, FLOYD C. "James Kirke Paulding and the Manuscripts
of William Byrd," MLN, LXVII (January), 56-57.
Reports on "the first printed criticism of Byrd's work,"
James Kirke Paulding's praise of the manuscript works of
Byrd in Letters from the South, 1817.

2   WILLIAMS, LLOYD HAYNES. "The Tragic Shipwreck of the Protes-
tant Switzers," WMQ, 3d ser. IX (October), 539-42.

(WILLIAMS, LLOYD HAYNES)
Byrd was particularly interested in attracting the Swiss
to settle his lands. To this end, he extolled the advantages of Virginia in the promotional tract Neu-gefundenes
Eden (1737) and in his correspondence with John Ochs, a
leader of Swiss immigrants. After a difficult voyage, the
immigrants who responded to Byrd's offer were shipwrecked
within sight of the intended port. Only 90 out of 300
survived this "stark, sheer tragedy" which "no recorded
Virginia shipwreck can approach."

1954 A   BOOKS - NONE

1954 B   SHORTER WRITINGS

1   HUBBELL, JAY B. "William Byrd" and "Bibliography," in The
       South in American Literature, 1607-1900. Durham, N.C.:
       Duke University Press, pp. 40-51, 919-21.
           Brief account of Byrd's life. Declares Byrd "everything
       a Virginia planter might become." Byrd ranks after Frank-
       lin and Edwards as a colonial writer. Discusses and evalu-
       ates Byrd's works; praises the History as his best work,
       the letters to Miss Smith as "an epistolary novel in mini-
       ature," and the "characters." Bibliography summarizes the
       history of publication of Byrd's works, including the lo-
       cation and use of manuscripts. Discusses variant editions
       and separate publications; lists periodical sources for
       letters, secondary sources of biographical information, and
       selected journal articles.

2   LEARY, LEWIS. "Byrd, William," in Articles on American Liter-
       ature, 1900-1950. Durham, N.C.: Duke University Press,
       pp. 34-35.
           Lists journal articles on Byrd from 1900-1950.

1955 A   BOOKS - NONE

1955 B   SHORTER WRITINGS

1   WRIGHT, LOUIS B. Culture on the Moving Frontier. Bloomington:
       Indiana University Press. Reprinted. New York: Harper
       and Row, 1961, pp. 22, 23-25, 28, 29, 170, 204.
           Credits the Byrd family with successful evolution.
       William Byrd II's "devotion to learning showed the nature
       of his...response to challenge." Byrd was "a persistent
       social climber." He had pleasure in his library and

1956

(WRIGHT, LOUIS B.)
rigorous scholarly self-discipline, and disrespected "those
who failed to meet the challenge." "Byrd...and most of
his class" believed "the Established Church was essential
to the civilization they wanted to perpetuate."

1956 A BOOKS - NONE

1956 B SHORTER WRITINGS

1   ADAMS, PERCY G. "The Real Author of William Byrd's Natural
       History of Virginia," AL, XXVIII (May), 211-20.
          Samuel Jenner claimed that the description of Virginia
       in his Neu-gefundenes Eden (1737) was by William Byrd.
       This work was edited by Beatty and Mulloy in 1940 as
       William Byrd's Natural History of Virginia. Demonstrates,
       by lining up parallel passages, that Jenner plagiarized
       this account from John Lawson's History of Carolina.

1957 A BOOKS - NONE

1957 B SHORTER WRITINGS

1   BRADFORD, ROBERT W. "William Byrd," in "Journey into Nature:
       American Nature Writing, 1733-1860." Ph.D. dissertation,
       Syracuse University, pp. 21-47.
          Byrd's literary works illustrate the growth of nature
       writing, for they "stand between the works of story-telling
       naturalists and the mental world of the virtuoso." Uses
       the History to explore Byrd's attitude toward people,
       wildlife, and the natural scene. Byrd goes to nature both
       for diversion and for its usefulness. He sees nature as
       an obstacle, but also in terms of "romantic" literary
       images.

2   WRIGHT, LOUIS B. The Cultural Life of the American Colonies,
       1607-1763. New York: Harper and Brothers, pp. 7-10,
       167-68, 209-10, 223-24.
          Briefly discusses Byrd's education, library, financial
       affairs, recreation, sexual interests, collection of
       paintings, scientific interests, and writings. The History
       is the "most urbane narrative of the colonial period."
       The humor and worldly attitude of the writer" contrast
       with most colonial writing.

1958 A   BOOKS - NONE

1958 B   SHORTER WRITINGS

1   WOLF, EDWIN, 2nd. "The Dispersal of the Library of William
           Byrd of Westover," PAAS, LXVIII (April), 19-106.
              The history of the dispersal of Byrd's library can be
           given in detail, because of the discovery of "some hundreds
           of volumes" of his books. The Westover library was sold
           to Isaac Zane in 1778. He sold the books in Philadelphia
           through an auctioneer and several agents. Some of the re-
           maining books were given to the Pennsylvania Hospital,
           others sold through booksellers. Most of the books appar-
           ently went to Philadelphians, and most of the located books
           are in Philadelphia institutions.
           Published separately by the University of Virginia Press,
           Charlottesville.

2   WRIGHT, LOUIS B. "The Life of William Byrd of Virginia, 1674-
           1744," in The London Diary, 1717-1721, and Other Writings,
           edited by Louis B. Wright and Marion Tinling. New York:
           Oxford University Press, pp. 3-46.
              A thorough and concise biography of Byrd's long life.
           Summarizes the broad chronological movement of the diary,
           analyzes the elements of private and public life Byrd em-
           phasized, and selects representative passages to convey
           the sense of life and drama in the best portions. Intro-
           duces Byrd's writings. Praises especially the History and
           the personal letters ("which often show careful literary
           craftsmanship").

1959 A   BOOKS - NONE

1959 B   SHORTER WRITINGS

1   FISHWICK, MARSHALL. "The Pepys of the Old Dominion," AH, XI
           (December), 5-7, 117-19.
              Byrd's "delicious" diaries "reveal a man who for candor,
           self-analysis, and wit is unsurpassed." His works cast
           light on Tidewater Virginia from 1700 to 1750, the for-
           gotten period in American history and literature. The
           manor house at Westover gives Byrd an important place in
           American architectural history.

2   LYNN, KENNETH S. Mark Twain and Southwestern Humor. Boston:
           Little, Brown and Co., pp. 7-22.

1960

    (LYNN, KENNETH S.)
      "The literature of . . . 'the Southwestern Tradition'
begins" with Byrd's History. Byrd daily acted out "the
drama of gentlemanhood." The Secret History is written in
"a blunt, jerky style, with a tough, unfooled directness
that seems unmistakably American." The History, in contrast, shows a "cooly sophisticated," amused, detached
narrator. From Byrd to the Civil War, humorists of the
Southwestern tradition used an elevated style to present
themselves as gentlemen.

3   WRIGHT, LOUIS B. "William Byrd, Citizen of the Enlightenment,"
in Anglo-American Cultural Relations in the Seventeenth and
Eighteenth Centuries; Papers Delivered at the Fourth Clark
Library Seminar, edited by Leon Howard and Louis B. Wright.
Los Angeles: University of California, pp. 26-40.
      Byrd was the "colonial counterpart of the European vir-
tuoso of the Enlightenment." Lists his writings and summarizes his life. Analyzes typical passages from the diary
to cast light on learning, public service, religion, sen-
suality, diet, and interest in natural history.

1960 A BOOKS - NONE

1960 B SHORTER WRITINGS

1   PARKS, EDD W. "William Byrd as Man of Letters," The Georgia
Review, XV (Summer), 172-76.
      Favorable general introduction to Byrd's prose. His de-
scriptions of Virginia and North Carolina are "written in
a clear and occasionally forceful style and with a constant
play of wit." Surveys the type of information revealed by
the diaries, with most attention to Byrd's reading prefer-
ences.

2   WRIGHT, LOUIS B. "William Byrd II: '...a Virginia Planter
of the Upper Class,'" in The Unforgettable Americans,
edited by John A. Garraty. New York: Channel Press,
pp. 36-40.
      Summary of Byrd's life. A "polished cavalier" with the
urbanity of London, he combined its dedication to literary
and scholarly pursuits with some of its vices. Byrd worked
hard at running his estate and at serving the colony as an
official. The secret diary is "one of the most fascinating
pieces of self-revelation surviving from the colonial
period."

WILLIAM BYRD II: A REFERENCE GUIDE

1961 A   BOOKS - NONE

1961 B   SHORTER WRITINGS

1   TROUBETZKOY, ULRICH. "Enough to Keep a Byrd Alive," <u>VC</u>, XI (Autumn), 36-41.
      Describes the dietary theories and eating habits revealed in Byrd's diaries. Culls passages to show typical meals, Byrd's food preferences, types of food eaten.

1963 A   BOOKS - NONE

1963 B   SHORTER WRITINGS

1   SALE, MARIAN M. "Westover's Col. Byrd," <u>Commonwealth</u>, XXX (January), 17-21, 47.
      General introduction to Byrd's life, character, writings. "This incredible English-bred Virginian" was equally at home in sophisticated England and on the frontier. Describes and prints photographs of architectural details of the mansion at Westover. Lists Byrd's writings (produced long before other Virginians wrote anything but propaganda). The diaries have made Byrd "another 'Pepys.'"

2   WRIGHT, LOUIS B., and MARION TINLING. "Introduction," in <u>The Great American Gentleman, William Byrd of Westover in Virginia</u> (<u>His Secret Diary for the Years 1709-1712</u>), edited by Louis B. Wright and Marion Tinling. New York: G. P. Putnam's Sons, pp. 3-7.
      A general account of Byrd's life. A summary of the contents of the extant portions of Byrd's diary, plus the history of their discovery and decoding. <u>The Great American Gentleman</u> abridges the earliest sections of the diary (1709-1712), which contains the fullest entries and is "particularly important for the information that it gives about social life in the colony."

1964 A   BOOKS - NONE

1964 B   SHORTER WRITINGS

1   GUMMERE, RICHARD M. "Byrd and Sewall: Two Colonial Classicists," <u>Transactions of the Colonial Society of Massachusetts</u>, LXII (February), 156-173.
      Compares and contrasts Byrd and Sewall, who were alike in their "main avocation ... an enthusiasm and a sound

1966

(GUMMERE, RICHARD M.)
knowledge of the ancient classics." Sewall's use of the
classics is "more personal, didactic and detailed" in contrast to Byrd's concealment of feeling, desire to entertain
(especially through satire) and brevity. The diaries show
Byrd's systematic reading of the classics. Sewall is
literal and Byrd allusive in the use of the classics.
Quotes some of the many classical allusions from the History. Byrd is "far more scholarly than he wishes us to
think, and takes his learning lightly."

2   MARAMBAUD, PIERRE. "Un Grand Planteur Virginien au XVIIIe
Siècle: William Byrd de Westover," Annales de la Faculté
des Lettres d'Aix-en-Provence, XXXVIII, no. 2, 367-79.
Byrd was a man of action who cultivated letters, and was
the idealized model of Virginians of the early eighteenth
century. Biography, using the diary for information on a
typical day. Quotes highlights from the History. Byrd
faithfully reproduces the atmosphere of a region and an
epoch. Byrd has been called "an American Pepys"; he also
shows the banter of the cavalier poets, humor of the
Restoration dramatists, and the elegant prose of Addison.

1966 A BOOKS

1   ROBERTSON, HENRY ALPHONSO, JR. "A Critical Analysis of
William Byrd II and His Literary Technique in The History
of the Dividing Line and The Secret History of the Line."
Ph.D. dissertation, University of Delaware.
Information from Byrd's letters, diaries, and the comments of contemporaries on Byrd's family background, life,
and public service. Detailed explanation of the history
of the boundary line dispute and sketches of the men who
served with Byrd on the commission. Summary of the trip.
Byrd's satirical comments on the Carolinians on the border
discussed in light of contemporary and later historians.
As naturalist, Byrd observed the resources of the region
with special interest in their practical use. General
survey of Byrd's writings with praise for him as writer of
humor and of satire.

1966 B SHORTER WRITINGS

1   LEONARD, KATHLEEN L. "Notes on the Text and Provenance of the
Byrd Manuscripts," Appendix in The Prose Works of William
Byrd, edited by Louis B. Wright. Cambridge, Mass.:
Harvard University Press, pp. 417-23.

1967

(LEONARD, KATHLEEN L.)

Discusses the discovery of the extant Byrd manuscripts of the History and the Secret History, and the history of acquisitions by the American Philosophical Society. Quotes from the correspondence between Thomas Jefferson and A.P.S.'s DuPonceau, who tried to collate the manuscript of the Secret History forwarded by Jefferson with the A.P.S.'s incomplete copy of the History. Describes an A.P.S. editor's bowdlerization of the History and quotes the recommendation that kept the Byrd manuscripts from being printed in the Transactions. Describes textual differences between copies of the Westover folio and A.P.S. octavo copies of the History; the revisions on the Westover copy, the basis of the present text, were probably Byrd's.

2   WRIGHT, LOUIS B. "Introduction: William Byrd as a Man of Letters," in The Prose Works of William Byrd of Westover, (Narratives of a Colonial Virginian), edited by Louis B. Wright. Cambridge, Mass.: Harvard University Press, pp. 1-38.

Surveys Byrd's extant writings, including an unpublished commonplace book, but excluding the diary. Emphasizes the content of the writings. Commends the "racy quality and idiomatic expression" of the History and Secret History and the satirical humor in most of Byrd's work. Byrd "remained essentially a dilettante of letters, albeit a brilliant one."

1967 A   BOOKS - NONE

1967 B   SHORTER WRITINGS

1   ADAMS, PERCY G. "Introduction to the Dover Edition," in William Byrd's Histories of the Dividing Line Betwixt Virginia and North Carolina, edited by William K. Boyd. New York: Dover Publications, Inc., pp. v-xxii.

Introduction to Byrd's life and writings (letters, diaries, other travel journals). Contrasts the History and the Secret History. The former provides a preliminary discussion of the boundary dispute; the latter uses fictional rather than real names for the characters, is franker (especially with regard to Byrd's own part in the expedition), is often "more dramatic" but also less full. The Secret History is full of Byrd's usual sexual wit. The two histories are "complementary." Byrd's style relies on parallelism and frequently heightens balance with alliteration and assonance.

1968

1968 A   BOOKS - NONE

1968 B   SHORTER WRITINGS

1   MILLAR, ALBERT EDWARD, JR.   "Spiritual Autobiography in Se-
            lected Writings of Sewall, Edwards, Byrd, Woolman, and
            Franklin: A Comparison of Technique and Content." Ph.D.
            dissertation, University of Delaware, pp. 142-60, 220-25,
            257-67.
              Admits Byrd can "barely" be included in a discussion of
            spiritual autobiography. However, Byrd often shows "in-
            trospective fears of divine vengeance" because of his
            failure to live an exemplary life. Points out the humorous
            linking of incongruous items such as Byrd's recording that
            he read a sermon immediately after "serving" his wife a
            "flourish." Byrd prayed almost daily, but the diaries
            seldom give information on the content or method of prayer.

1969 A   BOOKS - NONE

1969 B   SHORTER WRITINGS

1   CORE, GEORGE.   Review of The Prose Works of William Byrd of
            Westover, edited by Louis B. Wright. ArlQ, II (Summer),
            154-57.
              Wright's definitive edition of Byrd's major works is ex-
            cellent. Byrd's strengths are in his many resources of
            language and tone, his idiomatic diction, his narrative and
            dramatic skill. Like James Boswell, Byrd can "take large
            chunks of mundane fact and make them life-like and inter-
            esting." His prose is "the finest" in colonial America.

2   DAVIS, RICHARD B.   "Byrd, William (1674-1744)," in American
            Literature through Bryant, 1585-1830. New York: Appleton-
            Century-Crofts, pp. 24-25.
              Short list of selected primary sources, biography, and
            critical essays.

3   HATCH, ALDEN.   "Book Two: The Black Swan of Virginia," in
            The Byrds of Virginia. New York: Holt, Rinehart, and
            Winston, pp. 55-175.
              Detailed chronological account of Byrd's life: politi-
            cal service; propensity to "fall in love," and subsequent
            courtships and marriages; Evelyn (who died "in all proba-
            bility of boredom"); debts; land hunger; life in Virginia
            and England; writings; religion.

4   SCHMIDT-VON BARDELEBEN, RENATE. "Das Tagebuch des Kolonialen
        Sudens: William Byrd of Westover The Secret Diary," in
        Literatur und Sprache der Vereinigten Staaten: Aufsätze
        zu Ehren von Hans Galinsky, edited by Hans Helmcke, Klaus
        Lubbers, and Renate Schmidt-von Bardeleben. Heidelberg:
        Carl Winter Universitätsverlag, pp. 34-46.
            The individuality of Byrd's diary lies in the tireless
        recording of his days' routines without changing his de-
        scriptive manner. Compares Byrd to Sewall and Pepys. The
        theory of a break between Byrd's English writings (rhetori-
        cal, Baroque style) and his American writings ignores the
        diary, which already shows the "metaphor free, clear, short
        style" of the later American writings. Analyzes the style
        of the diary: verbs and auxiliary verbs play the greatest
        part; much ellipsis; a rhythm based on conjoined phrases,
        sound grouping through alliteration; often a three-beat
        structure.

5   WRIGHT, LOUIS B. "William Byrd (1674-1744)," in A Bibliog-
        raphical Guide to the Study of Southern Literature, edited
        by Louis D. Rubin. Baton Rouge: Louisiana State Univer-
        sity Press, pp. 162-63.
            Selected bibliography of editions of Byrd's works and
        secondary sources on him, 1866-1966.

1970 A BOOKS - NONE

1970 B SHORTER WRITINGS

1   INGE, M. THOMAS. "An Annotated Bibliography of William Byrd
        Scholarship, 1932-1969," in William Byrd of Westover, by
        Richard C. Beatty. Hamden, Conn.: Archon Books,
        pp. 231-40.
            Annotates briefly secondary sources on Byrd and publica-
        tions of his works from 1932-1969.

2   _____. "Preface, 1970 Edition," in William Byrd of Westover,
        by Richard C. Beatty. Hamden, Conn.: Archon Books,
        pp. xiii-xxx.
            Discusses Beatty's career as a biographer and praises
        his biography of Byrd. Comments on the primary material
        discovered since Beatty's work: the secret diaries, the
        letters and literary exercises. Characterizes and summar-
        izes the contents of the three portions of the diary.
        Byrd's letters and literary exercises "heighten his repu-
        tation as a gifted wit and man of talent." The new ma-
        terial enriches and expands but does not outdate or

1971

(INGE, M. THOMAS)
   contradict the picture of Byrd provided by Beatty
   (B1932.A1).

3   LEARY, LEWIS. "Byrd, William," in Articles on American
     Literature, 1950-1967. Durham, N.C.: Duke University
     Press, p. 44.
        Lists journal articles on Byrd from 1950-1967.

4   MARAMBAUD, PIERRE. "William Byrd of Westover: Cavalier,
     Diarist, and Chronicler," VMHB, LXXVIII (April), 144-83.
        As a writer, Byrd is "essentially an amateur." Surveys
     Byrd's cavalier writings: verse, character sketches and
     letters (sometimes very "entertaining"). Byrd's diary is
     significant as "a work of self-expression and a picture of
     eternal humanity" and of particular value as the only ex-
     tensive diary by an important Southerner. As literature
     it is disappointing and inferior to Pepys' diary. Ex-
     hibits many examples of humor from the three travel jour-
     nals. The History, Byrd's best work, "recalls Addison
     and his contemporaries" better than any other American
     work of Byrd's period.
        Reprinted, in expanded form, (B1971.A1).

5   NYE, RUSSEL B. "The Disposition of Virginia: William Byrd's
     Journal," in American Literary History: 1607-1830. New
     York: Alfred A. Knopf, pp. 90-94.
        Byrd's History is written in "an easy, urbane prose"
     equal to any American writer's (except Franklin's) before
     Irving. It "has a consistently acid tinge" because of his
     love for ridicule, and shows Byrd to be "a fine raconteur."

1971 A BOOKS

1   MARAMBAUD, PIERRE. William Byrd of Westover, 1674-1744.
     Charlottesville: University Press of Virginia.
        Critical biography. Part I: "Byrd's Life and Personal-
     ity." Because of his contradictions and good nature, Byrd
     "appears...far more attractive than most New England
     diarists." Part II: "Man of Letters." Discusses Byrd as
     virtuoso, cavalier author, diarist and chronicler. Con-
     cludes Byrd lacked "any marked intellectual originality"
     and only a small part of his works are "literary," though
     they are "social documents of extraordinary value." Part
     III: "Painter of Colonial Virginia": the plantation,
     colonial society, public life, the frontier, southern
     myth-making. Concludes Byrd enables us to distinguish his
     age from earlier and later eras in Virginia. A bibliography

(MARAMBAUD, PIERRE)
of primary and secondary sources, including Byrd's correspondence. Part II appeared in shortened form in VMHB
(B1970.B4).

1971 B   SHORTER WRITINGS

1   DOLMETSCH, CARL R.   "William Byrd II: Comic Dramatist?"   EAL,
       VI (Spring), 18-30.
          Presents evidence ("largely circumstantial") that Byrd
       may have been America's first comic dramatist.   In 1764,
       Col. Bolling reported that Byrd claimed to have collabor-
       ated on The Careless Husband.   The most significant evi-
       dence consists in a song, found in Notebook B, which may
       have been recorded before the premiere and publication of
       the play.   See also the correspondence between Sullivan
       and Dolmetsch (B1973.B2; B1973.B3).

1972 A   BOOKS - NONE

1972 B   SHORTER WRITINGS

1   ANON.   "Byrd, William II," in Virginia Authors, Past and
       Present, edited by Welford D. Taylor, et al.   Richmond:
       The Virginia Association of Teachers of English, pp. 19-20.
          A brief factual sketch of Byrd's life, and a selective
       list of Byrd's own works plus a few secondary sources.

2   DAVIS, RICHARD B.   "William Byrd: Taste and Tolerance,"
       Chapter 5 in Major Writers of Early American Literature,
       edited by Everett Emerson.   Madison: University of Wis-
       consin Press, pp. 151-77.
          A comprehensive yet concise study of Byrd as writer.
       Surveys Byrd's miscellaneous writings (prose and verse)
       and the diaries and letters.   Analyzes the letters for
       stylistic strengths and content; finds the "theme" of
       inner conflict between Byrd's identities as Englishman and
       American.   The History becomes "genuine epic," "a travel-
       adventure symbolic of the frontier experience."   Byrd's
       best prose is characterized by "antithesis; analogy; witty
       disparagement; puns; short, balanced, paradoxical, and
       epigrammatic statements."   Wit (usually irony which focuses
       on the lack of proportion in his world) is central to
       Byrd's vision.
       Reprinted in Literature and Society in Early Virginia,
       1608-1840 (B1973.B1).

1973

3   DOLMETSCH, CARL R. "William Byrd II: The Augustan Writer as
        'Exile' in His Own Country," VQR, XLVIII (Winter), 145-49.
        Review of Marambaud's biography of Byrd (1971). Praises
        it as a "major contribution," which should establish Byrd
        as a "belletrist." Marambaud's work is "solid, thorough
        and 'correct,'" but slights critical and comparative in-
        terpretation.

4   MEDEIROS, PATRICIA M. "Chapter V: William Byrd," in "The
        Literature of Travel of Eighteenth-Century America." Ph.D.
        dissertation, University of Massachusetts, pp. 109-66.
        The minor travel works and the diaries show Byrd's "in-
        tense interest in people." The Secret History and the
        History "really have little in common." The Secret History
        (which shows the influence of the drama) is chiefly de-
        voted to the portrayal of the commissioners and satirizing
        and criticizing people. The History is written to convey
        information; the "point of view" of a sophisticated London
        gentleman observing the American wilderness is central,
        and the contrast between aristocratic Virginia and the
        other colonies is an important theme.

5   SIMPSON, LEWIS P. "William Byrd and the South," EAL, VII
        (Fall), 187-95.
        Review of Marambaud's biography of Byrd (1971). Maram-
        baud's book is extolled as "capable" and "scholarly," but
        he does not recognize Byrd's significant role in develop-
        ing an aspect of American pastoralism—the Southern planta-
        tion as new Eden in which the gardeners were slaves and
        the master a "patriarch-philosophe." Byrd was "one of the
        makers of the slave society of the later American South."

1973 A BOOKS - NONE

1973 B SHORTER WRITINGS

1   DAVIS, RICHARD B. "William Byrd II: Taste and Tolerance,"
        in Literature and Society in Early Virginia, 1608-1840.
        Baton Rouge: Louisiana State University Press, pp. 97-132.
        Reprinted from Major American Writers of Early American
        Literature (B1972.B2).

2   DOLMETSCH, CARL R. "Response to Professor Sullivan," EAL,
        VIII (Spring), 89-90.
        Sullivan's contention (B1973.B3) that Notebook B is not
        in chronological order is probably correct; however, the

1974

(DOLMETSCH, CARL R.)
dating of the entry "A Song" is "at least coterminous with the first staging" of the play in which it appeared. Restates the possibility that Byrd may have composed the lyrics. See B1971.B1.

3   SULLIVAN, MAUREEN. "Letter to the Editor," EAL, VIII (Spring), 88-89.
Dolmetsch's evidence (B1971.B1) that Byrd may have composed a song used in Cibber's The Careless Husband is insufficient. Notebook B appears to be grouped by subject, rather than in chronological order; and Byrd was in London for the opening and publication of the play. These facts suggest Byrd copied the lyrics into his notebook from another source. See also Dolmetsch's reply (B1973.B2).

1974 A   BOOKS - NONE

1974 B   SHORTER WRITINGS

1   SPILLER, ROBERT E., et al., eds. "William Byrd II, 1674-1744," in Literary History of the United States: Bibliography. 4th ed., rev. New York: Macmillan Co., pp. 429-31, 882, 1156.
Lists editions of Byrd's works, biography and selected criticism, primary sources. Discusses location of manuscripts.

Writings About St. John de Crevecoeur, 1782 - 1974

1782 A BOOKS - NONE

1782 B SHORTER WRITINGS

1   ANON. "Art. I. Letters from an American Farmer," The Monthly
      Review; or, Literary Journal, LXVI-LXVII (June, August,
      October), 401, 140-46, 273-77.
          A series of extracts in three issues. The introductory
      material notes that Letters came out just when animosities
      between England and America were declining and interest in
      America was growing. "Internal evidence alone" should re-
      move all doubts as to the authenticity of the letters. In
      Crèvecoeur's book "truth and simplicity unite with good
      sense, to furnish the philosophic inquirer with rational
      amusement, and useful information."

2   ANON. "Letters from an American Farmer," The Gentleman's
      Magazine, LII (September, October), 439-41, 533-35.
          Crèvecoeur was an "ingenious and sentimental American
      husbandman...driven from a situation, the advantages and
      pleasures of which he describes with all that pathetic
      warmth of imagination with which we deplore lost happiness."
      The incident of the Negro in the cage (reprinted in this
      article) "must sensibly affect every mind not absolutely
      callous to the impression of humanity."

3   ANON. "London," Göttingsche Gelehrte Anzeigen: Gesellschaft
      der Wissenschaften zu Göttingen, II (7 December), 1201-4.
          Review of English version of Letters. To the reviewer
      it appears the principal intention of the author was to
      encourage emigration to America through descriptions of
      prosperity. Declares that the book was written more for
      lovers of light reading than for instruction. Doubts that
      the announced German translation will be successful because
      few readers will have the patience to separate the small
      amount of gold from the large amount of dross.

1783

4   ANON. Review of <u>Letters from an American Farmer</u>, <u>The European
       Magazine and London Review</u>, I (April), 272-78.
              A short introduction precedes extracts from <u>Letters</u>.
       Doubts the authenticity of the book because the writer
       seems to be "a man of cultivated and even refined mind"
       rather than a simple farmer. Speculates on there being two
       authors, one who observed America and one who wrote the
       book. <u>Letters</u> is interesting and instructive, "well fitted
       to afford matter of useful entertainment."

5   ANON. Review of <u>Letters from an American Farmer</u>, <u>The Scots
       Magazine</u>, XLIV (May), 263-64.
              A few sentences summarize the contents of <u>Letters</u>. Casts
       doubt on the book as authentic: it appears unsuitable "to
       the general character of an American, or indeed of any
       other farmer..." The account of the battle between two
       snakes is quite lively (an extract from it is quoted).

1783 A   BOOKS - NONE

1783 B   SHORTER WRITINGS

1   ANON. "Au Rédacteur du Courier de l'Europe, Sur l'Esclavage
       des Negroes," <u>Courier de l'Europe</u>, XIII (18 April), 245-48.
              Largely an argument against Negro slavery as unjust.
       Crèvecoeur, an eye-witness to slavery, causes tears of in-
       dignation. He describes the condition of free Negroes
       among the Quakers and in the northern provinces, as well
       as the horrible condition of Negroes elsewhere.
       Translated into Dutch in the <u>Algemeene Vaderlandsche Letter-
       Oefeningen</u> (C1783.B2).

2   ANON. "Brief aan den Uitgeever van <u>Le Courier de l'Europe</u> (*),
       over de Slaaverny der Negers," <u>Algemeene Vaderlandsche
       Letter-Oefeningen</u>, IV, part 2, 642-50.
              A Dutch translation of a letter first published in French
       (C1783.B3).

3   ANON. "<u>Lettres from an American Farmer</u>, &c. ou <u>Lettres d'un
       Fermier Américain</u>," <u>Courier de l'Europe</u>, XIII (14 March),
       167-68.
              Defends Crèvecoeur from Ayscough and others who attacked
       <u>Letters</u>. The style has led to suspicion of the authenti-
       city of the facts, but one should not expect a farmer to
       write like Gibbon. Praises the candor, ingenuity, and
       simplicity of the book. If it were fiction, it would be
       agreeable fiction.

4   ANON. "#156. Remarks on the Letters from an American Farmer,"
Gentleman's Magazine, LIII (December), 1036.
    Review of Ayscough's pamphlet on Crèvecoeur (C1783.B6).
Reviewer agrees that the author of Letters could not be a
farmer, many of his stories are "absurd and romantic" and
his "insidious" book is largely written to encourage emigration to America (which is therefore painted as "the
promised land").

5   ANON. Review of Remarks on the Letters from an American
Farmer, The Monthly Review; or, Literary Journal, LXVIII
(June), 536-37.
    Review of Ayscough's pamphlet attacking Letters
(C1783.B6). Reviewer agrees that Crèvecoeur intended to
"diffuse a spirit of migrating to America." Says Ayscough's remarks are pointed and sometimes just but some
are carried "farther than sound argument will bear."

6   AYSCOUGH, SAMUEL. Remarks on the Letters from an American
Farmer; or a Detection of the Errors of Mr. J. Hector St.
John; Pointing out the Pernicious Tendency of these Letters
to Great Britain. London: John Fielding.
    A pamphlet (twenty-six pages) attacking Letters as "a
new species of forgery," intended specifically to attract
emigrants. Crèvecoeur "would make an Irish hut appear a
palace most devoutly to be wished." "Exposes" Crèvecoeur
on the following points: (1) he was not born in America
as he pretends; (2) his literary style proves he never was
a farmer in America; (3) many things he says are false.
Crèvecoeur's errors of "fact" range from inconsistencies
of dates within the text to the "inconsistency" of keeping
hornets within his parlor.

7   LACRETELLE, PIERRE-LOUIS. "Lettre au Rédacteur du Mercure,"
Mercure de France (4 January), pp. 4-6.
    Introduces an extract from Letters and promises many
more. Crèvecoeur writes from a need to collect all that
moves him and not from a desire for publication. He lacks
the advantages of the trained writer, but his naïve paint-
ings, varied details, original manner compensate. Crèvecoeur's work, in addition to the great interest attached
to the subject, shines with all the beauties produced only
by natural poets, orators, and philosophers. Crèvecoeur's
own translation from English into French would best achieve
the poetry and elegance of the original.
    Reprinted in Lettres d'un Cultivateur Américain (C1784.B6).

1784

1784 A   BOOKS - NONE

1784 B   SHORTER WRITINGS

1   ANON. "Brieven van eenen Americaenschen Landman van Carlisle
        in Pensilvanien," <u>Algemeene Vaderlandsche Letter-Oefeningen</u>,
        I, part 1, 434-39.
        Several parts of <u>Letters</u> were translated and printed
        earlier in this journal. The response was highly favor-
        able. The book is worthwhile and shows internal signs of
        authenticity. Surveys contents of the twelve letters.
        Focuses on the description of Charleston and notes with
        pleasure that the American Revolution should change condi-
        tions there. Crèvecoeur speaks the language of nature and
        the heart.

2   ANON. <u>Maandelyksche Uittreksels of Boekzaal der Geleerde
        Wereld</u> [Amsterdam], (July), pp. 586-94.
        Review of Dutch translation of <u>Letters</u> (translated by
        F. A. Van der Kemp, Leyden, 1784). Summarizes the contents
        of the book. Furnishes a detailed account of Crèvecoeur's
        description of Charleston, especially the sufferings of
        the slaves.

3   [BRISSOT DE WARVILLE, JACQUES P.] "Letters from an American
        Farmer, <u>ou Lettres d'un Cultivateur Américain</u>," <u>Journal du
        Licée de Londres; ou Tableau de L'État Présent des Sciences
        et des Arts en Angleterre</u>, II (July), 286-87.
        Everything in these letters can be praised; love of hu-
        manity seems to have dictated them. Who is not transported
        by the simple pleasures of the Americans? To appreciate
        their happiness, one must be as simple and virtuous as they
        are. Upright, decent souls will read and reread it for
        amusement and instruction. Strong souls will discover a
        country where the wish of their heart is realized.

4   LACRETELLE, PIERRE-LOUIS. "Deuxième Lettre. Au Rédacteur du
        Mercure de France," in <u>Lettres d'un Cultivateur Américain,
        Écrites à W. S. Ecuyer, Depuis l'Année 1770, jusqu'à 1781.
        Traduites de l'Anglois par ***</u>. Vol. I. Paris: Chez
        Cuchet, pp. xxii-xxiv.
        Reprinted from <u>Mercure de France</u> (C1784.B5).

5   _____. "Lettre au Rédacteur du Mercure," <u>Mercure de France</u>
        (24 January), pp. 148-49.
        An unfortunate accident postponed the publication of
        <u>Lettres</u>. The manuscript was lost, but the book is now in
        press. The author writes with English liberty and

(LACRETELLE, PIERRE-LOUIS)
originality. The strangeness in his style should appeal
in a work which interests more by naïveté than by elegance.
Persons of the first merit have encouraged the author to
write in his own manner. The sweet tears that spill out
are touching homage to the author.
Reprinted in Lettres d'un Cultivateur Américain (C1784.B4).

6   ____. "Première Lettre. Au Rédacteur du Mercure de France,"
in Lettres d'un Cultivateur Américain, Écrites à W. S.
Ecuyer, Depuis l'Année 1770, jusqu'à 1781. Traduites de
l'Anglois par ***. Vol. I. Paris: Chez Cuchet, pp. vii-x.
Reprinted from Mercure de France (C1783.B7).

7   SCHREITER, KARL G. "Vorbericht," in Sittliche Schilderungen
von Amerika, in Briefen eines Amerikanischen Guthsbesitzers
an einen Freund in England, by St. John de Crèvecoeur.
Translated by Karl G. Schreiter. Leigniz and Leipzig:
David Siegert, pp. 3-6.
   Introduction to the German translation. Recommends the
book as of interest to more than statisticians and geog-
raphers. The book truly paints North American provinces
where Germans have become successful inhabitants. The
author is not a scholar but only an American farmer who reports what he has observed. His diction and expressions
are not those of a trained writer, but this is one of the
strongest evidences of the validity of the letters.

8   VAN DER KEMP, F. A. "Voorbericht van den Nederlandschen
Vertaelder," in Brieven van eenen Amerikaenschen Landman
van Carlisle in Pennsijlvaniën. Translated by F. A. Van
der Kemp. Leyden: L. Herdingh, pp. ix-xiii.
   Defends authenticity of Letters. Crèvecoeur is a
genuine countryman who knows what he is talking about and
who speaks the language of nature and the heart. Although
Crèvecoeur is a farmer, he has a precise, philosophical
literary style, due partly to the fact he has read works
by writers such as the Abbé Raynal. Crèvecoeur has a
creative and positive mind.

1785 A BOOKS - NONE

1785 B SHORTER WRITINGS

1   ANON. "Anécdote Tirée des Lettres d'un Cultivateur Américain,"
Journal de Paris, I (12 February), 179-81.
   Reprints the letter from Doctor M-ro, who loaned money
to a Virginia soldier. The introduction notes that the

1785

(ANON.)
    anecdote is so touching that readers should be grateful for
reading it in entirety.

2   ANON. "Belles-Lettres: Lettres d'un Cultivateur Américain,"
Journal de Paris, I (7 February), 157-59.
    Only someone who has lived in America like Crèvecoeur
can teach others about this vast country. He presents
nearly all imaginable aspects of the country in descriptions of vital interest. Reviewer summarizes Crèvecoeur's
description of the American, American prosperity, and the
geographical distinctions among settlers. America combines
the innocence and energy of a new people with the useful
knowledge of Europe.

3   ANON. "Geschichte. Paris, bey Cuchet: Lettres d'un Cultivateur Américain," Allgemeine Literatur-Zeitung, I (29
March), 297-99.
    Regrets the German translation (Sittliche Schilderung
von America, 1784) because it could prevent translation of
the letters added to the French edition. Few works have
such an attractive subject and so much nourishment for the
feeling heart. One can fill pages with anecdotes worthy
of note. The second volume contains statistical accounts
of the colonies. Discusses and quotes from Crèvecoeur's
account of the Indians, noting especially their decline
and the attractions of wilderness life.

4   ANON. "Lettre V. Lettres d'un Cultivateur Américain,"
L'Année Littéraire, II, 73-102.
    Lettres is an excellent work. Crèvecoeur is a good
citizen, a good farmer, a man of feeling and virtue who
speaks only of what he knows. There is hardly a subject
more interesting than America. The farmer dwells with
complacency on the prodigies of work done by the colonists.
He also pictures the horrors of the civil war. If it is
the greatest privilege of poetry to paint, one cannot re-
fuse to our cultivator the title of poet, and great poet.
His winter scene of the family is an honor to the paint
brush equal to the author of the Odyssey. Crèvecoeur's
work is an immense drama, full of interesting and pathetic
scenes. Recommends the book for the abundance of ideas,
sentiments, touching anecdotes.

5   ANON. "Lettre IV. Lettres d'un Cultivateur Américain,"
L'Année Littéraire, IV, 73-107.
    Asks a series of questions on Lettres: Why does such an
interesting work offer false views on religion? Why does

(ANON.)

the author have more pathetic than philosophical scenes in his book? The reviewer focuses on Crèvecoeur's descriptions of the Quakers, the Indians, the cruelties perpetrated by the English during the Revolution. Nantucket deserves comparison with the ancient republics of Greece. The philosopher should go to America to study men. Crèvecoeur is diffuse and repetitious. But he interests; he excites the passions very greatly. In his negligent, incorrect prose, strong and blazing, he shows the talent of a great poet.

6   ANON. "Lettres d'un Cultivateur Américain," Journal de Paris, I (10 February), 171-73.

The success of American farmers excites great interest. North America unites the innocence of the first centuries with the advantages of perfected reason. Reviewer summarizes the story of André and praises the Quakers. These agreeable pictures contrast with the horror-inspiring images of the civil war. The book is probably one of the great histories of North America. The style is often incorrect and is not exempt from declamation, but the author forcefully transports the reader to the scenes he describes.

7   ANON. "Lettres d'un Cultivateur Américain," L'Esprit des Journaux, III (March), 3-42.

The title alone promises interest because it is a book on America by an American. The reviewer praises America highly. Crèvecoeur is the poet of America as well as the historian. His sensitive soul and ardent imagination seize all striking scenes. Faults of style include frequent repetition and verbosity. But other more important qualities can be felt throughout: the sensibility and imagination of the style, original talent, not the art of effects but a valuable fidelity, a touching naïveté. The book deserves attention from poets as well as philosophers.

8   ANON. "Sittliche Schilderungen von Amerika, in Briefen eines Amerikanischen Guthsbesitzers," Allgemeine Deutsche Bibliothek, LXIII, 493-94.

Review of the German translation of Letters. Calls it a true mixture of sentimentality, description of areas in North America, remarks on natural history, on persons, places, customs. The book is full of improbabilities. The author is supposed to be a gentleman farmer who has barely learned to read, but the letters at times show fine phrases, Latin sentences, and bombast. The description of the island of Nantucket, which makes up a large part

1785

(ANON.)
    of the book is good and entertaining. In the third letter,
    there is an enticing invitation to America; however, a
    poor immigrant seldom has true good fortune there.

9   LACRETELLE, PIERRE-LOUIS. "Nouvelles Littéraires: Fin de
       l'Extrait des Lettres d'un Cultivateur Américain," Mercure
       de France (29 January), pp. 202-21.
           Largely extracts from Lettres. Praises the sentiments
       and manners, the simple and sublime virtue in the book.
       Relates stories of Crèvecoeur's aid to escaped American
       prisoners of war and Crèvecoeur's reunion with his
       children after the Revolution.

10   _____. "Nouvelles Littéraires: Lettres d'un Cultivateur
       Américain," Mercure de France (22 January), pp. 150-170.
           The title alone promises interest because the book is
       written by an American on America. Crèvecoeur's book of-
       fers instruction on a nation with pure and simple manners.
       The book is the poetry of America as well as its history.
       Crèvecoeur's sensitive soul and ardent imagination catch
       all striking scenes. Indians and Negroes especially merit
       interest, but it is the author himself whom one always
       discovers with new pleasure. Crèvecoeur lacks art but has
       natural talent. Surveys contents of the book and quotes
       lengthy extracts.

11   [MEISTER, JAKOB H.] "Lettres d'un Cultivateur Américain," in
       Correspondence Littéraire, Philosophique et Critique par
       Grimm, Diderot, Raynal, Meister, Etc., edited by Maurice
       Tourneux. Vol. IV. Reprint. Paris: Garnier Frères,
       1880, pp. 88-89.
           Lettres is written without method or art, but with much
       interest and sensibility; the book fulfills perfectly the
       author's intention of making the reader like America and
       recognize its advantages. Crèvecoeur is too detailed,
       repetitious, and wordy, but he attracts by simple and
       true paintings, by the expression of an honest soul pro-
       foundly appreciative of domestic virtues and the sweetness
       of independence. The book strongly encourages emigration.
       Some of the author's remarks on the Indians would make
       Rousseau happy.

1786 A BOOKS - NONE

1786 B SHORTER WRITINGS

1   BRISSOT DE WARVILLE, JACQUES P. Examen Critique des Voyages
         dans l'Amérique Septentrionale de M. le Marquis de Chas-
         tellux. Paris and London.
             An attack on Chastellux and defense of Lettres. Chas-
         tellux was a soldier who scorned the Quakers for being
         pacifists. Declares that Chastellux was writing to refute
         Crèvecoeur's picture of the Quakers. Supports Crèvecoeur's
         sympathetic account of the Quakers and eulogizes Lettres.
         Translated and published as A Critical Examination of the
         Marquis de Chastellux's Travels...translated from the
         French...with Additions and Corrections of the Author,
         Philadelphia: Joseph James, and London (C1788.B4).

1787 A BOOKS - NONE

1787 B SHORTER WRITINGS

1   ANON. "Extraits. Belles-lettres," Journal de Paris, II
         (17 August), 1003-5.
             Of all the works on North America, Lettres has had most
         success because of the author's singular talent for com-
         munication and lively feeling for the grand spectacle of
         America. In spite of errors and prolixity, he interests
         and sometimes makes the tears run. One believes his re-
         citals and likes believing them. Relates the story of
         Fellowes' aid to Crèvecoeur's children.

2   ANON. "Lettres d'un Cultivateur Américain," Mercure de
         France (7 July), pp. 46-47.
             We have been the first to respond to the merit of Lettres,
         a work of originality. Its success has justified our
         eulogies. Undoubtedly this carefully executed and enlarged
         edition will be greeted with eagerness.

3   ANON. "Paris, bey Cuchet: Lettres d'un Cultivateur Améri-
         cain," Allgemeine Literatur-Zeitung, IV (9 October), 74-79.
             The 1787 (French) edition of Lettres improves and en-
         larges the 1782 edition. Crèvecoeur paints with the
         liveliest colors the patriarchal circumstances of Ameri-
         cans. His descriptions are often very moving. He de-
         scribes the poor emigrant who becomes a well-to-do planter
         in a few years. He also pictures distress with lively

1788

(ANON.)
colors. Selects particularly interesting articles:
Andrew the Hebridean, the tales of Warner Mifflin, the
"anecdote of the Indian dog." A substantial part of the
article furnishes factual information on particular American states as gleaned from Lettres.

1788 A BOOKS - NONE

1788 B SHORTER WRITINGS

1   BRISSOT DE WARVILLE, JACQUES P. "Continuation de la Lettre
          sur l'Ouvrage des États-Unis," Analyse des Papiers Anglois,
          II (April), 337-44.
          Crèvecoeur speaks little of Europe but he has truly de-
        scribed European deprivation, egotism, and vanity. Mazzei
        (C1788.B8) objects to the praise given to the botanist
        Bertrand [sic], but Crèvecoeur lauds those who deserve
        praise. Mazzei believes the detailed pictures of the in-
        habitants of Nantucket lack interest, but who can remain
        insensitive to the charms of Nantucket culture? The in-
        cident of the Negro in the cage (which Mazzei declares
        false) is not extraordinary in terms of the cruelty given
        slaves.
        Reprinted in Réponse (C1788.B6), pp. 8-14.

2   _____. "Continuation de la Lettre sur l'Ouvrage des États-
          Unis," Analyse des Papiers Anglois, II (April), 362-68.
          It is easier to believe Crèvecoeur was deceived about
        the incident of the Negro in the cage than to imagine him
        inventing such atrocities. Mazzei (C1788.B8) attacks
        Crèvecoeur's affection for the Quakers, but this affection
        grew out of long observation and true rapport. Summarizes
        the arguments defending Crèvecoeur in the previous two
        letters (C1788.B1, B5).
        Reprinted in Réponse (C1788.B6), pp. 14-20.

3   _____. "Continuation de la Lettre sur l'Ouvrage des États-
          Unis," Analyse des Papiers Anglois, II (April), 385-92.
          Declares he is not blind to the faults of Letters.
          Crèvecoeur's greatest fault is his enthusiasm; he exag-
        gerates because of his sensitive soul, benevolence, and
        strong imagination. The fault is not dangerous because
        Crèvecoeur focuses on pure and virtuous objects. If Crè-
        vecoeur exaggerates, it is because of his enthusiasm for
        domestic and rural life and for America, and he can be
        forgiven. Attacks Mazzei's criticism of the Quakers.
        Reprinted in Réponse (C1788.B6), pp. 20-27.

1788

4   (BRISSOT DE WARVILLE, JACQUES P.) A Critical Examination of
       the Marquis de Chastellux's Travels...translated from the
       French...with Additions and Corrections of the Author.
       Philadelphia: Joseph James, and London.
       See the original version (C1786.B1).

5   _____. "Lettre de M. Brissot de Warville aux Rédacteurs de
       l'Analyse des Papiers Anglois," Analyse des Papiers Ang-
       lois, II (April), 312-20.
           Quotes his previous judgments on Crèvecoeur's letters;
       "The love of humanity has dictated them." Defends Crève-
       coeur by refuting Mazzei's strictures (C1788.B8) point by
       point. Mazzei has attempted to involve Crèvecoeur in the
       general censure against authors who have written on Ameri-
       ca. Mazzei calls Crèvecoeur an ignorant Pennsylvanian who
       knows little of other parts of America, is stupefied by
       mediocre and common things, and knows little about Europe.
       But Crèvecoeur, who lived twenty-five years in the United
       States, knows the country well, and is not describing
       Europe.
       Reprinted in Réponse (C1788.B6), pp. 1-7.

6   _____. Réponse à une Critique des Lettres d'un Cultivateur
       Américain, des Quakers, &c. Faite par l'Auteur Anonyme
       des Recherches sur les États-Unis. Paris: n.p.
           Reprinted in Analyse des Papiers Anglois, (C1788.B1-B3,
       B5).

7   GÖTZE, AUGUST E. "Vorrede des Uebersetzers," in Briefe eines
       Amerikanischen Landmanns an den Ritter W.S. in den Jahren
       1770 bis 1781. Aus dem Englischen ins Französische von
       *** und Jetzt aus dem Französischen Übersetzt und mit
       Einigen Anmerkungen Begleitet von Johann August Ephraim
       Götze, erstem Hofdiaconus der St. Servatii-Kirche zu
       Quedlinburg. Translated by A. E. Götze. Leipzig: Sieg-
       fried Lebrecht Crusius, I, pp. iii-vi.
           Götze's whole heart was stirred by the French version of
       Lettres. The previous German translation (Sittliche Schil-
       derungen von Amerika, 1784) was not based on the revised
       and enlarged French edition. Götze does not know whether
       many incidents are exaggerated or invented, but the heart
       itself speaks for the truth of the book, and the scenes of
       nature and of the Indians appear genuine. Even if they
       were deceptions, the morals and humanity of the work would
       not be lost. Götze has translated freely, not always hold-
       ing himself to Crèvecoeur's often inflated style. All
       readers who value humanity, virtue, morals, nature will be
       grateful for this enchanting book.

1801

8   MAZZEI, FILLIPO. <u>Recherches Historiques et Politiques</u> sur
     <u>les États-Unis de l'Amérique Septentrionale Par un Citoyen</u>
     <u>de Virginie</u>. Vol. IV. Paris: Froullé, pp. 98-102.
        Warns that the manners described in <u>Letters</u> are not
     general in America. Crèvecoeur paints only the manners of
     those on the frontier; in the interior of the country the
     manners of life largely resemble those of Europe. Many
     people formed false ideas by reading this book. Crève-
     coeur represents himself as a man who lives on the frontier,
     is astounded at common things, and judges without objects
     of comparison. He thus resembles a young villager who re-
     gards his schoolmaster as the first philosopher of the
     earth.

1801 A BOOKS - NONE

1801 B SHORTER WRITINGS

1   A[NDRIEUX, FRANÇOIS]. "Littérature.--Voyages," <u>Revue Philoso-</u>
     <u>phique, Littéraire et Politique</u>, (8 August), pp. 280-90.
        Review of <u>Voyage</u>. The device of the discovered manu-
     script allows an irregular and varied form. Quotes ex-
     tensively from a debate between two Indian chiefs over the
     advantages and disadvantages of civilization. Declares
     that Crèvecoeur's enchanting pictures of the United States
     seem to resolve the question of how to reach the middle
     point most beneficial to man between the extremes of
     savagery and civilization. Analyzes the meaning of "equal-
     ity" as used in <u>Voyage</u>.

2   ANON. "Foreign Literature, Article I," in <u>Appendix to the</u>
     <u>Monthly Review, Enlarged</u>, XXXVI (January), 449-64.
        Review of <u>Voyage</u>. The book is "a collection of informa-
     tion drawn from various sources." Reviewer gives most at-
     tention to the "most entertaining" descriptions of Indians,
     objecting to Crèvecoeur's declaration that they are an in-
     ferior race. Crèvecoeur's principal intention is "to de-
     scribe new settlements, and lands in their first state of
     improvement." He did not "fetter himself by method." Some
     parts of the book are too close to <u>Letters</u>, and the author
     sometimes "falls into a species of sentimental declama-
     tion." These are slight defects, for the book is enter-
     taining.

3   LA HARPE, JEAN F. DE. "Lettre CCXIII," in <u>Correspondance</u>
     <u>Littéraire Addressée à Son Altesse Impériale Mgr. le Grand-</u>

1801

(LA HARPE, JEAN F. DE.)
Duc, Aujourd'hui Empereur de Russie. Vol. IV. Paris:
Migheret, pp. 278-81.
Lettres is the most interesting and most instructive of
all the works published on North America. The translation
is often incorrect and anglicized, but Crèvecoeur shows no
affectation. He paints only what he has seen and felt.
The book stresses the rights natural to man, which have
been engraved in the soul of an American farmer, perhaps
the most liberated man on earth. The part of the work
which treats the Indians is especially interesting.

4   TROUVÉ, CHARLES-JOSEPH. "Voyages: Voyage dans la Haute-
Pennsylvanie et dans l'État de New York," Gazette Nationale
ou le Moniteur Universal, nos. 205, 207 (25 and 27 Germinal
an 9), pp. 863-64, 871.
As in Lettres, the reader encounters warmth of imagination, animated style, picturesque descriptions, indignation
against vice, a profound sensitivity, a sincere love of
all that contributes to happiness. The true goal of this
interesting book is to show the advantages of civilization
over the savage life. Focuses on Crèvecoeur's treatment of
the Indian, depiction of the progress of civilization in
America, examination of American foundations and institu-
tions, the character of George Washington.

5   V., B. "Voyage dans la Haute-Pensylvanie et dans l'État de
New-Yorck," Mercure de France, no. XXI (21 April),
pp. 193-202.
Readers will find Voyage even more instructive than
Lettres. We cannot cite the least part of what deserves
to be extracted. Speculates on the reasons for the passionate love of gain and mercantile spirit among the
colonists. Crèvecoeur shows man exerting great force
against nature to obtain success. He has truly observed
society in its origin and in a state of progress. The
artifice of the discovered manuscript frees the author to
abridge and lengthen to avoid boredom. The reader can
open the book with confidence.

6   _____. "Voyage dans la Haute-Pensylvanie, par S. J. de
Crèvecoeur," Mercure de France, no. XXII (6 May),
pp. 265-75.
What reader will not be instructed by the information
Crèvecoeur gives on all aspects of the Indians? Quotes
several extracts on the Indians, selected to prove the
superiority of society over the state of nature. Crèvecoeur's thoughts on whether America can preserve its

1802

(V., B.)
   happiness or will decay appear profound and reasonable,
   but he deserves most praise for having collected facts on
   the present and past.

1802 A   BOOKS - NONE

1802 B   SHORTER WRITINGS

1   TIEDEMANN, DIETERICH. "Vorrede," in Reise in Ober-Pensyl-
       vanien und im Staate Neu-York von einem Adoptirten Mit-
       gliede der Onéïda-nation. Herausgegeben von dem Verfasser
       der Briefe eines Amerikanischen Landwirthes, by Crèvecoeur.
       Translated by Dieterich Tiedemann. Berlin: Voss, 1802,
       pp. iii-xiv.
          Introduction to German translation of Voyage. At times
       the whole seems to be nothing but a fictional voyage. But
       the detailed descriptions prove that the author has seen
       America or is using accounts from someone who has. The
       descriptions of places, landscape, natural scenery, speech
       of the Indians, and statistical reports appear to be re-
       liable. Only the journey, the many discussions, and the
       person of Hermann seem fictional. The book is of interest
       for its nature scenes (painted with exceptional skill) and
       the information on America. The style is often too senti-
       mental and clamorous, and has been tempered through
       omissions.

1808 A   BOOKS - NONE

1808 B   SHORTER WRITINGS

1   BOUCHER DE LA RICHARDERIE, G. Bibliothèque Universelle des
       Voyages. Vol. VI. Paris: Treuttel et Würtz, pp. 61-63.
          Includes a biographical sketch of Crèvecoeur. The many
       anglicisms in Lettres give it more energy. A sensitive
       soul truly feels the heroic perseverance of the Americans.
       Scenes of devastation contrast with more tender scenes.
       The anecdotes are touching little dramas. One learns the
       most interesting ideas on North America, and no other
       writer knows the Indians so well. Crèvecoeur's partiality
       for the Quakers is excusable because of their estimable
       qualities.

1813 A BOOKS - NONE

1813 B SHORTER WRITINGS

1   ANON. Journal de l'Empire, V (21 November), 225.
             Funeral eulogy for Crèvecoeur, who died at 82. He was
         the author of Letters and of several very esteemed works
         on rural economy and politics. Praises his sensibility,
         imagination, vast knowledge. He gave more than twenty
         years to public service, working particularly to encourage
         agricultural improvements. Voyage includes touching epi-
         sodes, and glimpses of practical morality that reveal
         Crèvecoeur's virtuous heart. Lists his many distinguished
         friends and the members of his family.
         Reprinted in Robert de Crèvecoeur, pp. 290-92 (C1883.A1).

1818 A BOOKS - NONE

1818 B SHORTER WRITINGS

1   BRISTED, JOHN. The Resources of the United States. New York:
         James Eastburn, pp. 4-5.
             Gilbert Imlay and Crèvecoeur (in Letters and Voyage)
         "exceedingly exaggerated" the condition of the United
         States, describing it as "the abode of more than all the
         perfection of innocence, happiness, plenty, learning, and
         wisdom, than can be allotted to human beings to enjoy."

1829 A BOOKS - NONE

1829 B SHORTER WRITINGS

1   [HAZLITT, WILLIAM.] "Sermons and Tracts," Edinburgh Review,
         L (October), 130-31.
             Remarks on Crèvecoeur included in a review of Channing's
         Sermons and Tracts. Letters gives "not only the objects,
         but the feelings of a new country." The battle between
         the two snakes has "an Homeric gravity and exuberance of
         style." Crèvecoeur's account of the people of Nantucket
         shows an admirable ability to identify with them: "This
         power to sympathize with nature, without thinking of our-
         selves or others, if it is not a definition of genius,
         comes very near to it." Crèvecoeur has a "liberal, un-
         affected style." The most interesting part of the book
         describes the beginnings of the American war.

1855

1855 A BOOKS - NONE

1855 B SHORTER WRITINGS

1   DUYCKINCK, EVERT A., and GEORGE L. DUYCKINCK. "Hector St.
       John Crèvecoeur," in Cyclopaedia of American Literature.
       Vol. I. New York: Charles Scribner. Reprinted. Detroit:
       Gale Research Company, 1965, pp. 183-87.
              Letters is "one of the most pleasing and agreeable" of
       the books in which an intelligent and sensitive European
       describes life in early America. It is "all sentiment
       and susceptibility in the French school of St. Pierre and
       Chateaubriand, looking at homely American life in the
       Claude Lorraine glass of fanciful enthusiasm."

1878 A BOOKS - NONE

1878 B SHORTER WRITINGS

1   MARSHALL, O. H. "Preliminary Note" to "Description of the
       Falls of Niagara," by Crèvecoeur, Magazine of American
       History, II (October), 604-13.
              Voyage, "a curious mosaic of romance and reality, written
       in a florid, though pleasing style and well worthy of
       perusal," is valuable primarily for its notes on the his-
       tory and resources of the country. Crèvecoeur's "graphic
       description" of Niagara Falls in its "primeval grandeur"
       is published here for the first time.

1880 A BOOKS - NONE

1880 B SHORTER WRITINGS

1   MARSHALL, O. H. "Notes: Hector St. John de Crèvecoeur--
       Supplementary Notice," Magazine of American History, IV
       (June), 453-54.
              Marshall believes Crèvecoeur and the man with the same
       name who served in the French war in America were "un-
       doubtedly identical." He presents the following evidence:
       (1) the men who recommended the cadet for a lieutenancy
       were intimate friends of the writer's family; (2) no other
       member of the Crèvecoeur family could possibly have served
       in the French colony; (3) family documents show the writer
       passed many years in Canada; (4) Crèvecoeur exhibits per-
       sonal knowledge of the country which was the subject of
       controversy; (5) the title on a map drawn by the officer
       is written in the writer's handwriting.

1883 A   BOOKS

1   CRÈVECOEUR, ROBERT DE. Saint John de Crèvecoeur, Sa Vie et
       Ses Ouvrages, 1735-1813. Paris: Librairie des Biblio-
       philes.
          The first full-length biography of Crèvecoeur, written
       by his great-grandson. Crèvecoeur's own papers (especially
       his correspondence) and Crèvecoeur family documents form
       the basis for a detailed account of Crèvecoeur's personal
       life. Letters and Voyages are often used as though they
       were autobiographical. The appendix prints extracts from
       Crèvecoeur's letters, family documents, documents dealing
       with Crèvecoeur's role in creating the packet service, his
       correspondence on steam navigation, his memoir of Mme.
       d'Houdetot, a bibliography of primary and secondary
       sources. Describes Crèvecoeur's manuscripts; notes many
       had not yet been published.

1883 B   SHORTER WRITINGS – NONE

1897 A   BOOKS – NONE

1897 B   SHORTER WRITINGS

1   TYLER, MOSES COIT. "Two Apostles of Quietness and Good Will:
       John Woolman and St. John Crèvecoeur," in The Literary
       History of the American Revolution, 1763-1783. Vol. II.
       New York: G. P. Putnam's Sons. Reprinted. New York:
       G. P. Putnam's Sons, 1900, pp. 347-58.
          Lengthy quotations illustrate the "two distinct notes--
       one of great peace, another of great pain" in Letters.
       Most of the book is a "prose pastoral" praising life in
       the New World.

1904 A   BOOKS – NONE

1904 B   SHORTER WRITINGS

1   LEWISOHN, LUDWIG. "Introduction," in Letters from an American
       Farmer. New York: Fox, Duffield and Co., pp. ix-xxv.
          Letters was often republished in the eighteenth century
       but neglected in the nineteenth century. Now Americans
       show a new interest. Sketches Crèvecoeur's life. He was
       "typically French, since there were in him no extremes of
       opinion or emotion." Letters is "primarily...a piece
       of literature." Crèvecoeur believed he had found the
       "land of plain living and high thinking, of simple virtue

1906

(LEWISOHN, LUDWIG)
and untrammeled manhood," which satisfied his resistance
to institutional restraints. The ideal was the Indian
living in simplicity. Crèvecoeur's English prose style
shows "unusual delicacy." His French writings are un-
important.

2   TRENT, W. P.   "Prefatory Note," in Letters from an American
       Farmer. New York: Fox, Duffield and Co., pp. v-viii.
          Trent persuaded the publishers to reprint Letters.
       Little new biographical information has been found on
       Crèvecoeur except letters from Mme. d'Houdetot to Crève-
       coeur (printed in this volume). Crèvecoeur's ideal Ameri-
       can strongly influenced Americans for more than a century.
       Crèvecoeur's work as a lover of nature will be appreciated
       today. Letters is "a book worth reading for its own sake."

1906 A BOOKS - NONE

1906 B SHORTER WRITINGS

1   ANON. "January Meeting, 1906," Proceedings of the Massachu-
       setts Historical Society, 2d ser. XX, 20-21.
          Franklin B. Sanborn presented a photograph (reproduced
       with the article) of Crèvecoeur's farmhouse and grounds
       from an aquarelle drawn by Crèvecoeur. He then read a
       letter by the widow of Robert de Crèvecoeur. Speaking of
       Crèvecoeur's extant and lost papers, she declared that
       manuscripts of the works published by the "American
       Farmer" were lost during the French Revolution.

2   SANBORN, F. B. "The 'American Farmer' St. John de Crèvecoeur
       and His Famous 'Letters' (1735-1813)," PMHB, XXX, 257-86.
          Supplies an account of Crèvecoeur's life taken largely
       from Robert de Crèvecoeur's biography. Crèvecoeur was
       little known at this time. His writings in both French
       and English are "a far more valuable contribution to
       American history, topography and social conditions, from
       1757 to 1800, than any other contemporary author." Com-
       mends the "general accuracy" of Crèvecoeur's description
       of America and his "artless style."

1912 A BOOKS - NONE

1912 B SHORTER WRITINGS

1   BLAKE, WARREN B. "Introduction," in Letters from an American
       Farmer. New York: E. P. Dutton, pp. vii-xxiii.
          Crèvecoeur's life was "filled...with romantic inci-
       dent." Biographical account which focuses on the many
       shifts of fortune experienced by this "eighteenth-century
       Thoreau." Sees two qualities in Letters: Crèvecoeur's
       naïveté and his "essential modernity." "Crèvecoeur's
       honest and unconventionalized love of his rural environ-
       ment is great enough to bridge the difference between the
       year 1782 and the present."

2   _____. "Some Eighteenth-Century Travellers in America," The
       Dial, LII (1 January), 5-9.
          High praise to Crèvecoeur's work. Letters is "litera-
       ture." Crèvecoeur shows "the tone of an idealistic
       philosopher and the powers of observation of a woodsman."
       He "lived a kind of pastoral poetry," and saw American
       nature directly, rather than through literature. He is
       "the eighteenth-century Thoreau...a French-American
       Thoreau."

1915 A BOOKS - NONE

1915 B SHORTER WRITINGS

1   BOYNTON, PERCY H. "A Colonial Farmer's Letters," The New
       Republic, III (19 June), 168-70.
          Letters shows a "typically American" optimism that pre-
       cludes awareness of the problems implicit in the nation's
       westward expansion, its growth of population through im-
       migration, its future industrialization, and even pre-
       cludes full awareness of the problems resulting from
       slavery. Crèvecoeur nevertheless deserves credit for
       foreseeing such developments in the future of the U.S.

1916 A BOOKS

1   MITCHELL, JULIA POST. St. Jean de Crèvecoeur. New York:
       Columbia University Press.
          Detailed, factual biography. Attempts to answer ques-
       tions about Crèvecoeur's early life that stem primarily
       from his inconsistency about dates. Supplies evidence for

1917

(MITCHELL, JULIA POST)
both sides of the chief biographical puzzle: did Crèvecoeur fight in Canada under Montcalm? Concludes (errone-
ously) that he did not. Especially detailed on Crèvecoeur's
work as French Consul: the packet service he initiated,
his efforts to develop trade between the countries, his
promotion of scientific projects. A chapter on Crèvecoeur
as an "agriculturalist" (supplemented by an account of his
"Agricola" papers). Crèvecoeur's letters are a chief
primary source.

1916 B SHORTER WRITINGS - NONE

1917 A BOOKS - NONE

1917 B SHORTER WRITINGS

1   COOPER, LANE. "Travellers and Observers, 1763-1846," in The
        Cambridge History of American Literature, edited by William
        P. Trent et al. Vol. I. New York: G. P. Putnam's Sons.
        Reprinted. New York: The Macmillan Co., 1946, pp. 198-201.
          Summary of Crèvecoeur's life; a brief, factual survey of
        the contents of the twelve essays of Letters.

1918 A BOOKS - NONE

1918 B SHORTER WRITINGS

1   CHINARD, GILBERT. L'Exotisme Américain dans l'Oeuvre de
        Chateaubriand. Paris: Hachette, pp. 20-21.
          French public opinion endowed American rebels with the
        virtues of the innocent savages of the New World. No work
        contributed more to this confusion than Letters. This
        book also praised the Quakers and pious and hard-working
        American farmers. For Crèvecoeur, true happiness was re-
        alized by the Indians, who were as imposing as Roman
        senators.

1919 A BOOKS - NONE

1919 B SHORTER WRITINGS

1   BOYNTON, PERCY H. "Crèvecoeur, the 'American Farmer,'" in A
        History of American Literature. Boston: Ginn and Co.,
        pp. 59-68.

(BOYNTON, PERCY H.)
Stresses Crèvecoeur's optimism, which was fed by a vision of an America that seemed to possess unlimited resources. Crèvecoeur resembles Thoreau; the "artistic strain" in Crèvecoeur expressed itself best through descriptions of nature.

2   LAWRENCE, D. H. "Studies in Classic American Literature (iii) Henry St. John de Crèvecoeur," The English Review, XXVIII (January), 5–18.
Crèvecoeur "had his dynamic being" in the "sensual" rather than "spiritual" consciousness. Crèvecoeur identified himself as "a child of Nature" and exemplified (as American Farmer) the life prescribed by "French romantic idealists." As artist, however, Crèvecoeur "glimpsed some of the passional dark mystery." Praises highly Crèvecoeur's vision of insects, birds, and snakes "in their own pristine being." Crèvecoeur "wanted to know as the Indians and savages know, darkly, and in terms of otherness," but he was also determined to believe that nature is "sweet and pure." Hence his resolution to live with the savages is a "swindle."
Reprinted (C1962.B2); revised version (C1923.B1).

1923 A   BOOKS - NONE

1923 B   SHORTER WRITINGS

1   LAWRENCE, D. H. "Hector St. John de Crèvecoeur," in Studies in Classic American Literature. New York: Seltzer, pp. 32–49.
Shortened version of the essay published in The English Review (C1919.B2). The introductory discussion on duality has been cut from the original. The second halves of the two essays are similar in content, but this version shows a tone of playful humor rather than the serious tone of the original. In discussing Crèvecoeur's account of Indian captives, Lawrence concludes that Indians sometimes look like white men while the reverse is never true, whereas the original essay declared the opposite is true.

1924

1924 B SHORTER WRITINGS

1   EMERSON, OLIVER F. "Notes on Gilbert Imlay, Early American
           Writer," PMLA, XXXIX (June), 400-39.
               Quotes a letter from Mary Wollstonecraft that proves
           Imlay knew Crèvecoeur. Speculates on when they first be-
           came acquainted. Points out "certain likenesses" between
           Letters and Imlay's Description: the epistolary form, the
           praise for the new country, the similar number of letters
           (twelve and eleven), letter nine written in opposition to
           slavery.

2   HICKS, PHILLIP M. "II: The Beginnings of the Natural History
           Essay," in "The Development of the Natural History Essay
           in American Literature." Ph.D. dissertation, University
           of Pennsylvania, pp. 30-38.
               Letters shows Crèvecoeur's appreciation for the life of
           the American farmer. Letter two shows the "seemingly un-
           studied progression of ideas appropriate to the out-door
           essay." Crèvecoeur possessed the qualities "indispensable"
           to the natural history essayist: "the eye to observe and
           the imagination to interpret." In prose, Crèvecoeur and
           Gilbert White "mark the beginning of a period of apprecia-
           tion of Nature."

1925 A BOOKS - NONE

1925 B SHORTER WRITINGS

1   BISSELL, BENJAMIN. "The American Indian in English Litera-
           ture of the Eighteenth Century," YSE, LXVIII, 46.
               Crèvecoeur's Letters reveals a sentimental longing for
           the state of nature and "a certain melancholy poetic color-
           ing." The book shows not only the wish for freedom and
           independence, but also "romantic longings for solace in
           nature, peace in escaping the restlessness of civilized
           life."

2   BOURDIN, HENRI L. "The Crèvecoeur Manuscripts," in Sketches
           of Eighteenth-Century America, edited by Henri L. Bourdin,
           Ralph M. Gabriel, and Stanley T. Williams. New Haven:
           Yale University Press, pp. 14-24.
               Bourdin relates how he discovered Crèvecoeur's manu-
           scripts (preserved by descendants in France). Describes
           the manuscripts, lists the essays included among them, and

1925

(BOURDIN, HENRI L.)
discusses the information they give on dating Crèvecoeur's works. About two-thirds of Crèvecoeur's American writing (including his loyalist essays) were not included in Letters.

3   BOURDIN, HENRI L., and STANLEY T. WILLIAMS. "Crèvecoeur on the Susquehanna," YR, XIV (April), 552-84.
"The most important and perhaps most interesting" of Crèvecoeur's English writings are the unpublished manuscripts kept in the family archives in France (from which the extracts here printed were taken). Traditional judgments of Crèvecoeur as "a stalwart patriot" and "a utopian dreamer" need reexamination.

4   _____. "Crèvecoeur the Loyalist, The Grotto: An Unpublished Letter from the American Farmer," The Nation, CXXI (23 September), 328-30.
"The Grotto," a description of a refuge for Tories fleeing persecution by American patriots, proves Crèvecoeur "was basically a loyalist."

5   _____. "The American Farmer Returns," The North American Review, CCXII (September-November), 135-40.
One of the authors discovered Crèvecoeur's unpublished manuscripts in France. Crèvecoeur pictures the farmer's "cheerful routine" (largely social and domestic pleasures), in many of these manuscripts. The many "winter-pieces" contrast with the sunny pastorals in Letters. The harshly realistic pictures of frontier life frequently found in the unpublished manuscripts also contrast with Letters.

6   _____. "The Unpublished Manuscripts of Crèvecoeur," SP, XXII (July), 425-32.
Crèvecoeur's life and writings must be reexamined because of the large number of unpublished manuscripts discovered by Bourdin. Lists the title and length of each essay, and describes the appearance of the manuscripts. For the first time, Crèvecoeur's own handwriting and the corrections in the first edition ("ruthlessly" made by someone other than Crèvecoeur) are available. Allusions to Canada in the papers prove Crèvecoeur stayed there before going to New York.

7   FÄY, BERNARD. "Bibliographie Critique des Ouvrages Français Relatifs aux Etats-Unis, 1770-1800," in Bibliothèque de la Revue de Littérature Comparée. Vol. VII. Paris: E. Champion, 64.

1926

(FÄY, BERNARD)
Letters was accepted as giving the true image of the
United States. Crèvecoeur's works were among the most
frequently cited (in both French and American journals).
Letters has warmth and eloquence, but unfortunately is
sometimes too naïvely optimistic.

8   GABRIEL, RALPH H. "Crèvecoeur and His Times," in Sketches of
        Eighteenth-Century America, edited by Henri L. Bourdin,
        Ralph H. Gabriel, and Stanley T. Williams. New Haven:
        Yale University Press, pp. 1-13.
            The previously unpublished letters of Crèvecoeur in this
        book are significant because they depict "fairly completely"
        the life of the country family. Crèvecoeur was a talented
        observer who really knew America and depicted it realis-
        tically. He was the "forerunner" of other writers who
        have portrayed American farm life, such as Riley and Hamlin
        Garland.

9   WILLIAMS, STANLEY T. "Crèvecoeur as a Man of Letters," in
        Sketches of Eighteenth-Century America, edited by Henri L.
        Bourdin, Ralph H. Gabriel, and Stanley T. Williams. New
        Haven: Yale University Press, pp. 25-35.
            Crèvecoeur was primarily a man of action rather than a
        "literary man." His style has "vigor and freshness" and
        a convincing simplicity. Crèvecoeur showed "unique powers
        as a writer," primarily in the short narratives or descrip-
        tions in Letters.

1926 A BOOKS - NONE

1926 B SHORTER WRITINGS

1   BOURDIN, HENRI L., and STANLEY T. WILLIAMS. "Hospitals
        [During the Revolution]: An Unpublished Essay by J. Hector
        St. John Crèvecoeur," PQ, V (April), 157-65.
            Introduction to an essay by Crèvecoeur. Although some-
        times inaccurate and untrustworthy, Crèvecoeur's study of
        America is "irreplaceable." For he was a participant in
        American farm life and also in the "political and reli-
        gious confusion of the age." He was an epitome of the
        real pioneer caught by conflicting loyalties.

2   _____. "Sketch of a Contrast between the Spanish and English
        Colonies," University of California Chronicle, XXVIII
        (April), 152-63.

(BOURDIN, HENRI L....)
Introduces an essay found among the unpublished manuscripts of Crèvecoeur discovered by Bourdin. The new
letters reveal Crèvecoeur as a "patient observer" and a
"thoughtful student" of America. Crèvecoeur often writes
about religion; the subjoined essay is significant not for
what he says of Spanish customs but for what he says of the
American religion he knew.

3   MOORE, JOHN B. "Crèvecoeur and Thoreau," Papers of the Michi-
     gan Academy of Science, Arts and Letters, V, 309-33.
     The "surface resemblance" between Crèvecoeur and Thoreau
     is misleading. Crèvecoeur was the "American Rousseau,"
     and also "a kind of French Franklin," who busily promoted
     many projects. The social and diplomatic side of Crève-
     coeur's life also differs from Thoreau's solitude. Thoreau
     believed there was virtue in direct contact with nature,
     while nature appealed to Crèvecoeur largely because of the
     "bright idea of property." Crèvecoeur's work is relatively
     superficial.

4   WILLIAMS, STANLEY T. "American Spirit in Letters," in Pageant
     of America. Vol. XI. New Haven: Yale University Press,
     pp. 61, 97.
     Presents a brief sketch of Crèvecoeur's life. He is a
     naturalist, "an eighteenth century Thoreau" with a romantic
     strain. In Sketches he presents realistic pictures of
     frontier life; "Landscapes" reveals he was a staunch Tory.

1927 A BOOKS - NONE

1927 B SHORTER WRITINGS

1   MOORE, JOHN B. "The Rehabilitation of Crèvecoeur," SR, XXXV
     (April), 216-30.
     The publication of Sketches (1925) "rehabilitated" Crève-
     coeur. Letters presents a sentimental and panic-stricken
     American farmer. Sketches gives a better picture of the
     life of a colonist than any other book. The loyalist
     sketches are "the most effective work of the imagination"
     written in America during the period. Crèvecoeur works
     best in short, descriptive narratives and dramatic episodes.
     "Landscapes," Crèvecoeur's one attempt at drama, is his
     most significant and best work.

2   PARRINGTON, VERNON L. "The Frontier: Land of Promise," in
     Main Currents in American Thought: The Colonial Mind.

1930

(PARRINGTON, VERNON L.)
Vol. I. New York: Harcourt, Brace and Company. Reprinted.
New York: Harcourt, Brace and World, 1954, pp. 143-50.
Crèvecoeur perhaps knew more about the French and English
colonies as a whole than anyone in his age. He based his
Letters on solid "economic fact" by describing how an environment of abundant natural resources offered opportuni-
ties for economic individualism and consequently produced
both the "new American psychology" and American institu-
tions.

1930 A BOOKS - NONE

1930 B SHORTER WRITINGS

1   LOCK, D. R. "Crèvecoeur: An Early North American Classic,"
       Dublin Review, CLXXXVI (April-June), 291-97.
       Crèvecoeur promotes a "mild" version of eighteenth-
       century primitivism. Praises his style and thought as
       characteristically French: he exhibits "ease and fluency,
       the effortless making of a point," and his "reason is never
       swamped in a flood of rhetoric." Crèvecoeur has a talent
       for describing nature.

2   W[ILLIAMS], S[TANLEY] T. "Crèvecoeur," in Dictionary of
       American Biography, edited by Allen Johnson. Vol. III.
       New York: Charles Scribner's Sons, pp. 542-44.
       Traces Crèvecoeur's remarkable life. A "master of the
       pioneer farm," Crèvecoeur gives a detailed picture of
       colonial farming. The loyalist Crèvecoeur also gives a
       "sane" picture of the Revolution. He expressed his "warm
       humanity" in essays written in the "simple strong writing"
       characteristic of eighteenth-century America.

1932 A BOOKS - NONE

1932 B SHORTER WRITINGS

·1   LEWISOHN, LUDWIG. "Beginnings," in Expression in America.
       New York: Harper and Brothers, pp. 36-38.
       Crèvecoeur was an "artist" and "thinker." His "idylls"
       were the first literary expression of "that great hope of
       a new start for mankind which...fired the hearts of
       thousands of immigrants..."

1933 A BOOKS

1   RICE, HOWARD C. Le Cultivateur Américain: Étude sur l'Oeuvre
      de Saint John de Crèvecoeur. Paris: Champion.
         An authoritative study of the stages of development of
      Letters and of the influence of the book. Biographical
      sketch. Studies the changes in Letters through the follow-
      ing stages: (1) the manuscript; (2) the English edition,
      1782; (3) the French edition, 1784; (4) the French edition
      in three volumes, 1787. Also provides a detailed study of
      Crèvecoeur's contemporary reputation; many editions and
      translations, reviews and extracts attest to the popularity
      of the book in Europe. Studies Letters as an interpreta-
      tion of America: Crèvecoeur's picture of slavery, his pro-
      gressively more idealized treatment of the Indians, his
      changing attitude toward the Revolution, his depiction of
      American realities and the American dream. A valuable
      bibliography lists primary sources (including manuscripts,
      translations, reprintings) and secondary sources.

1933 B SHORTER WRITINGS - NONE

1934 A BOOKS - NONE

1934 B SHORTER WRITINGS

1   RICE, HOWARD C. "The American Farmer's Letters, With a Check-
      list of the Different Editions," The Colophon, Part XVIII.
         A compact discussion of the chief topics of Rice's book
      (C1933.A1). Most attention is given to the "life-story"
      of Letters from manuscript through English and French edi-
      tions. The English edition (1782) shows the optimistic
      "man of feeling." The French editions (1784, 1787) are
      more sentimental and literary. English and French editions
      were popular.

1935 A BOOKS - NONE

1935 B SHORTER WRITINGS

1   PATTEE, FRED L. "The Emerging West," in The First Century of
      American Literature, 1770-1870. New York: Cooper Square
      Publishing, pp. 149-53.
         Letters has "vividly realistic" pictures of the American
      frontier and Sketches includes "gruesomely truthful" ac-
      counts of the Revolution. Sketches contains passages of

1938

(PATTEE, FRED L.)
    prose unequaled by any American writer before Irving.
Crèvecoeur was a "sentimentalist" and "dreamer" who described American life as an idyll. Today he is valuable
only for the "touches of realism" that grew out of genuine
observation.

1938 A BOOKS - NONE

1938 B SHORTER WRITINGS

1   SHELLEY, PHILIP A. "Crèvecoeur's Contribution to Herder's
        'Neger-Idyllen,'" JEGP, XXXVII (January), 48-69.
          Cites German reviews of Letters to prove that it was
widely known in eighteenth-century Germany. German aboli-
tionists in particular were interested in Crèvecoeur's
description of slavery and often reprinted his anecdotes.
Hence Herder's "Neger-Idyllen" (from Briefe zu Beförderung
der Humanität), which resembles Letters in its "gospel of
humanitarianism," versifies two stories from Letters: the
Negro in the cage, and the kind treatment of a Negro by
the Quaker Warner Mifflin.

1939 A BOOKS - NONE

1939 B SHORTER WRITINGS

1   MASTERSON, JAMES R. "The Tale of the Living Fang," AL, XI
        (March), 66-73.
          Letter ten of Letters includes the story of a rattlesnake
fang embedded in a boot that kills two men. The story has
the qualities of a tall tale: concern for plausibility;
told by a first-hand witness; told to an outsider interested in American marvels. There is a long tradition of
similar stories about this snake.

1943 A BOOKS - NONE

1943 B SHORTER WRITINGS

1   RICE, HOWARD C. "Introduction," in Saint-John de Crèvecoeur,
        Qu'est-ce qu'un Américain? Princeton: Princeton Univer-
        sity Press, pp. 1-13.
          Introduction to Crèvecoeur's life and to the English and
French versions of Letters. Discusses environmental and

1947

(RICE, HOWARD C.)
literary influences operating upon Crèvecoeur and also the influence of his book on European thought. By discovering happiness in America, Crèvecoeur expressed the American dream. "What is an American?" shows Crèvecoeur's usual combination of personal observation and philosophical digression, and is the most "characteristic" essay he ever wrote.

1946 A BOOKS

1   ADAMS, PERCY G. "Crèvecoeur's 'Voyage dans la Haute Pensylvanie et dans l'État de New York.'" Ph.D. dissertation, University of Texas.
Adams discusses the geography of Voyage; flora and fauna; Crèvecoeur's treatment of the Indian (the subject which receives most attention in the dissertation); Voyage as history; as literature; its relationship to other travel literature. Adams' published articles (See C1947.B1; C1948.B1; C1949.B1; C1953.B1; C1961.B1; C1962.B1) succinctly summarize his conclusions on the above topics, except geography and flora and fauna. Ferreting out Crèvecoeur's sources (acknowledged and unacknowledged) was a primary object of the dissertation. Concludes that Crèvecoeur was a "romanticist" in literary style and depictions of nature and the Indian. Voyage deserves "a major place" among Crèvecoeur's works, because of its value as history.

1946 B SHORTER WRITINGS - NONE

1947 A BOOKS - NONE

1947 B SHORTER WRITINGS

1   ADAMS, PERCY G. "Crèvecoeur and Franklin," Pennsylvania History, XIV (October), 273-79.
In Voyage, Crèvecoeur misleadingly cited Franklin as a source for information. One such passage was actually taken from Jonathan Carver. A speech Crèvecoeur attributed to Franklin (long accepted as genuine by Franklin's biographers) was taken from Gilbert Imlay. A passage supposedly from a conversation between Crèvecoeur and Franklin came from a paper Franklin read to the American Philosophical Society.

1948

2   EISINGER, CHESTER E.   "The Freehold Concept in Eighteenth-
       Century American Letters," WMQ, 3d ser. IV (January),
       42-59.
            According to the "freehold concept," status and economic
       security come from owning property. Although Crèvecoeur's
       description of the immigrant's "exaltation in ownership"
       seems romantic, Crèvecoeur also acknowledged the "solid
       economic core" of freehold agriculture. Crèvecoeur "made
       the definitive statement on the relation between ownership
       of land and independence."

1948 A BOOKS - NONE

1948 B SHORTER WRITINGS

1   ADAMS, PERCY G.   "Notes on Crèvecoeur," AL, XX (November),
       327-33.
            Voyage contains a number of chapters attributed to in-
       correct sources. The information for a paper attributed
       to a Mr. B* (describing Indian mounds) came from William
       Bartram's Travels. Crèvecoeur abridged and "embellished"
       Dr. William Smith's account of an expedition against the
       Indians and also assigned this narration to a fictitious
       participant.

1949 A BOOKS - NONE

1949 B SHORTER WRITINGS

1   ADAMS, PERCY G.   "Crèvecoeur--Realist or Romanticist," The
       French American Review, II (July-September), 115-34.
            Like all of Crèvecoeur's writings, Voyage includes both
       realistic observation and romantic success stories and
       descriptions of nature. Voyage has romantic elements new
       to Crèvecoeur: descriptions of wild nature (particularly
       mountain scenery), Indian legends and tales, account of
       Gothic ruins, the melancholy tone to a number of the his-
       tories, the utopian element in the pictures of America.
       Concludes that Crèvecoeur was "essentially a romanticist."
       The chapter on Crèvecoeur as a writer in Adams' disserta-
       tion (C1946.A1) presents the same conclusion.

2   EISINGER, CHESTER E.   "Land and Loyalty: Literary Expressions
       of Agrarian Nationalism in the Seventeenth and Eighteenth
       Centuries," AL, XXI (May), 160-78.

136

1952

(EISINGER, CHESTER E.)
The chance to obtain a freehold and the act of acquiring it (a process described in Letters) changed the immigrant into an American. Crèvecoeur "makes the most enthusiastic and the fullest statement of agrarian nationalism in his time."

1951 A BOOKS - NONE

1951 B SHORTER WRITINGS

1   MURDOCK, KENNETH B. "Woolman, Crèvecoeur, and the Romantic Vision of America," in The Literature of the American People: An Historical and Critical Survey, edited by Arthur H. Quinn. New York: Appleton-Century-Crofts, pp. 129-33.
        Introduction to Crèvecoeur's life and writings, with stress on his literary style. Crèvecoeur's English style was "uneven" but at times shows "genuine and intense feeling." Crèvecoeur's best passages describe simple pleasures of the country. He is "often highly skillful in his use of evocative detail."

2   REY, LÉON. "Crèvecoeur and the First Franco-American Packet Line," translated by Kent Foster. New York Historical Society Quarterly Bulletin, XXXV (April), 171-94.
        Crèvecoeur was the "father" of the first Franco-American Packet line (a fleet of vessels that transported mail and passengers during the years from 1783 to 1788). He was instrumental in establishing the service, showed zeal in efforts to encourage and improve it and great dismay when it was terminated.

1952 A BOOKS

1   ARMSTRONG, HAROLD C. "The Significance of Crèvecoeur's Letters from an American Farmer and Sketches of Eighteenth Century America in the Pastoral Literary Tradition and in the Literary Polemic of Revolutionary America." Ph.D. dissertation, University of Washington.
        Crèvecoeur's pastoralist sketches of American colonial life (generally, the earliest letters he wrote) show an ideal society with the four qualities of peace, simplicity, order, contentment. Pastoral elements include the use of simple people, the love of nature, purification by contact with nature, "natural law," the "self-regulating" society

1953

(ARMSTRONG, HAROLD C.)
with harmony among all classes. Crèvecoeur was a loyalist.
His praise of American superiority was a form of "quiet
agitation for peace and English sovereignty."

1952 B SHORTER WRITINGS - NONE

1953 A BOOKS - NONE

1953 B SHORTER WRITINGS

1   ADAMS, PERCY G. "The Historical Value of Crèvecoeur's Voyage
        Dans La Haute Pensylvanie et Dans New York," AL, XXV (May),
        152-68.
            Voyage is valuable as history. It offers more interpre-
        tation of historical motives and movements than Crevecoeur's
        previous works. Crèvecoeur anticipated Turner's 1890 de-
        scription of the development of new farming districts.
        Voyage supplies much information on farm customs and the
        surveying of frontier lands. In contrast to his earlier
        works, Crèvecoeur describes mostly wealthy farmers, but
        Voyage is also "the first published book of its kind" to
        treat extensively the difficulties of farm life in America.

2   PEARCE, ROY HARVEY. The Savages of America: A Study of the
        Indian and the Idea of Civilization. Baltimore: Johns
        Hopkins Press, pp. 139-43.
            Crèvecoeur did not find Utopia among civilized men, and
        hence he created a noble savage. Letters shows a desire
        for a return to nature and also a desire for the best of
        civilized life. Written largely for Europeans, Letters
        shows Crèvecoeur's effort "to simplify the American accord-
        ing to the European dream."

1954 A BOOKS - NONE

1954 B SHORTER WRITINGS

1   LEARY, LEWIS. "Crèvecoeur, J. Hector St. John," in Articles
        on American Literature, 1900-1950. Durham, N.C.: Duke
        University Press, p. 64.
            Lists journal articles on Crèvecoeur from 1900-1950.

1957 A BOOKS - NONE

1957 B SHORTER WRITINGS

1   BEWLEY, MARIUS. "The Cage and the Prairie: Two Notes on
        Symbolism," HudR, X (Autumn), 403-14.
             The incident of the Negro in the cage in Letters is so
        "intensely real" because it acquires symbolic status. The
        cage becomes a symbol of "metaphysical nightmare," and the
        Negro himself a symbol of the "terrible cost of merely man-
        made order." Analyzes the details that contribute to the
        symbol: the movement of the air, caused by birds of prey
        rather than (merciful or gentle) rain; the "sacramental
        echo" of the insects feeding on the flesh and drinking the
        blood. The "polite and measured prose," which reflects
        the illusion of external order, contrasts ironically with
        the hideous reality of the caged man.
        Reprinted in The Eccentric Design (C1959.B1).

2   BRADFORD, ROBERT W. "Crèvecoeur," in "Journey into Nature:
        American Nature Writing, 1733-1860." Ph.D. dissertation,
        Syracuse University, pp. 81-113.
             Letters is "a new genre--nature writing," which merges
        the letter form, Rousseauistic and rationalistic philosophy,
        travel literature, botany and natural history. Letters
        shows the interest in people and in marvels of natural his-
        tory typical of travel literature. Examines the literary
        characteristics and themes of Letters. Crèvecoeur presents
        the type, not the individual, but foreshadows the attitude
        toward nature of the next century. Crèvecoeur's American
        farmer values a "natural" style of writing.

1959 A BOOKS - NONE

1959 B SHORTER WRITINGS

1   BEWLEY, MARIUS. "Symbolism and Subject Matter," in The Ec-
        centric Design. New York: Columbia University Press,
        pp. 102-6.
             Reprinted from HudR (C1957.B1).

1961

1961 A BOOKS - NONE

1961 B SHORTER WRITINGS

1   ADAMS, PERCY G. "Introduction," in Crèvecoeur's Eighteenth-
         Century Travels in Pennsylvania and New York. Translated
         and edited by Percy G. Adams. Lexington: University of
         Kentucky Press, pp. xiii-xliv.
             Introduction to selections translated from Voyage ("in
         many ways Crèvecoeur's most important, certainly his most
         pretentious book"). Discusses Voyage as travel book, as
         history, as literature, Crèvecoeur's "peculiar plagiar-
         isms." Much of the information is found in Adams' earlier
         works (C1946.A1; C1947.B1; C1948.B1; C1949.B1; C1953.B1).
         Adds new information on the Indian stories and legends
         in the book. Characterizes Crèvecoeur's "new style" in
         Voyage ("better arrangement of thoughts...smoother sen-
         tences," and frequent use of figures of speech).

2   ANON. "Crèvecoeur's Hartford Diploma," Connecticut Historical
         Society Bulletin, XXVI (April), 40-44.
             In 1785, Hartford, Connecticut, extended "the Freedom of
         the City" to Crèvecoeur and his two sons. The Connecticut
         Historical Society has letters from Crèvecoeur describing
         the award. The article includes pictures and a transcrip-
         tion of the award. In 1784 New Haven granted citizenship
         to Crèvecoeur, his sons and his daughter.

3   FAIRCHILD, HOXIE N. The Noble Savage: A Study in Romantic
         Naturalism. New York: Russell and Russell, pp. 100-104,
         375-76.
             Crèvecoeur is "one of the first real Americans" and also
         "a Frenchman steeped in the philosophy of nature." Letters
         shows a "Ben Franklin-like morality" of cheerfulness and
         industry, but also an admiration for life close to nature.
         Crèvecoeur's Indians are close to nature, and white men
         who live with them are reluctant to return to civilization.
         Voyage (which gives much favorable and unfavorable informa-
         tion on the Indian) reverses Crèvecoeur's earlier attitude
         by attacking the idealization of the Indian.

4   LYNDENBERG, JOHN. "American Novelists in Search for a Lost
         World," Revue des Langues Vivantes, XXVII, 306-21.
             A discussion of American novelists, prefaced by comments
         on Crèvecoeur's essay "What is the American, this new man?"
         Crèvecoeur's question has been basic to the "imaginative
         focus" of most major American novelists. For Crèvecoeur,
         the American dream was "simple and all but a present re-
         ality."

1962

1962 A   BOOKS - NONE

1962 B   SHORTER WRITINGS

1   ADAMS, PERCY G.   "After Defoe," and "St. Jean de Crèvecoeur or
        Benjamin Franklin?" in Travelers and Travel Liars, 1660-
        1800. Berkeley: University of California Press,
        pp. 129-31, 158-61.
            Voyage is one of the "most confusing" of the "pseudo
        travel books" because Crèvecoeur relied heavily upon other
        writers yet cited the wrong sources. Analyzes in detail
        (as typical of the methods used by Crèvecoeur and other
        "fireside travelers") Crèvecoeur's erroneous attributions
        to Franklin and also Crèvecoeur's use of William Smith's
        history. The following works by Adams also treat Crève-
        coeur's sources (C1946.A1; C1947.B1; C1948.B1; C1961.B1).

2   LAWRENCE, D. H.   "Hector St. John de Crèvecoeur," in The
        Symbolic Meaning: The Uncollected Versions of Studies in
        Classic American Literature, edited by Armin Arnold. Font-
        well, Arundel, England: Centaur Press, pp. 53-70.
            Reprints the essay published in The English Review
        (C1919.B2). See also the revised version (C1923.B1).

3   STONE, ALBERT E., JR.   "Crèvecoeur's Letters and the Be-
        ginnings of American Literature," Emory University Quar-
        terly, XVIII (Winter), 197-213.
            American literature "begins" with Letters, which is
        "literary, modern, and characteristically American."
        Crèvecoeur anticipated many characteristics of American
        literature: the provincial persona, the American scene as
        subject matter, the use of idyl or melodrama, the border-
        line as location, alienation and disorder as themes, unre-
        solved polarities instead of resolution. Letters drama-
        tizes "the conflict between belief and experience" by
        showing an American Eden and also "the desperate struggle
        to hold on to that vision." "Crèvecoeur's characteristic
        voice is statement by metaphor and fable; it is parable
        moving in the direction of myth." Analyzes specific pas-
        sages to show Crèvecoeur's "myth-making imagination." A
        version of this essay is used as foreword to Letters
        (C1963.B2).

1963

1963 A BOOKS - NONE

1963 B SHORTER WRITINGS

1   CHYET, STANLEY. "Lewisohn and Crèvecoeur," Chicago Jewish
       Forum, XXII, 130-36.
          Lewisohn's introduction to the 1904 edition of Letters is
       especially interesting because it reveals much about Lewi-
       sohn himself. Lewisohn admired Crèvecoeur's "humanness
       and joie de vivre," "whimsey," "serenity," "good sense and
       sound judgment." Lewisohn (who grew up in the South)
       criticized Crèvecoeur's condemnation of slavery. Other-
       wise, Lewisohn's view of Crèvecoeur was "compassionate and
       accepting...where possible, he avoided anything but virtue
       in Crèvecoeur."

2   STONE, ALBERT E., JR. "Foreword," in Letters from an American
       Farmer; and Sketches of Eighteenth-Century America. New
       York: New American Library, pp. vii-xxvi.
          A version of the essay printed in Emory University
       Quarterly (C1962.B3).

1964 A BOOKS - NONE

1964 B SHORTER WRITINGS

1   BOSTELMANN, CLARISSA SPENCER. "Biographical Sketch and Trans-
       lator's Foreword," in Journey into Northern Pennsylvania
       and the State of New York, by Crèvecoeur. Translated by
       Clarissa S. Bostelmann. Ann Arbor: University of Michigan
       Press, pp. vii-xii.
          Crèvecoeur wrote Voyage to bolster his position as an
       authority on America. The book describes "an agrarian
       Utopia" of landed gentry. Crèvecoeur's word choice is
       often "whimsical"; his sentences are usually very long.
       Although much is "sheer declamation," Crèvecoeur's eight-
       eenth-century style is "rhetoric, often pure and often
       complex."

2   MARTZ, LEO. The Machine in the Garden: Technology and the
       Pastoral Ideal in America. New York: Oxford University Press.
       Reprinted. New York: Oxford University Press, 1968,
       pp. 107-16.
          The literal achievement of the pastoral ideal in America
       is "the controlling theme" of Letters. The American land-
       scape, by giving settlers their own land, awakens them to
       a "new consciousness" and "secular resurrection." Not wild
       nature, but the "middle landscape," midway between the

142

1969

(MARTZ, LEO)
  extremes of the frontier and civilization, is the ideal.
  Letters is "a simple-minded book" since Crèvecoeur saw
  America as a refuge from historic change.

3   PLOTKIN, N. A. "Saint-John de Crèvecoeur Rediscovered:
     Critic or Panegyrist?" FHS, III (Spring), 390-404.
       The traditional view of Crèvecoeur as "a sort of literary
     Watteau" comes from Letters. Crèvecoeur's realistic analy-
     sis of American defects is found in Sketches. These "two
     faces" are not really contradictory. The essays in Letters
     were selected to support the Whig cause. The "gilded de-
     scription" of America made Letters a work of revolutionary
     import which greatly stimulated European criticism of the
     existing social order.

1967 A BOOKS - NONE

1967 B SHORTER WRITINGS

1   RAPPING, ELAYNE A. "Theory and Experience in Crèvecoeur's
     America," AQ, XIX (Winter), 707-18.
       Letters and Voyage begin with "hypothetical acceptance"
     of America as a society exemplifying "a neat theoretical
     model": agrarian democracy is the ideal social structure,
     midway between savagery and overly complex civilizations.
     But both books are "circular," for progress is illusionary.
     The implicit movement is toward "the truly natural Indian
     who offers a version of reality more secure, more rational,
     and more consistent than the models." The Indian, however,
     is merely "another fictitious model of reality" used as a
     contrast to American society.

1969 A BOOKS

1   AGEE, WILLIAM H. Chapters 5-8 in "Franklin and Crèvecoeur:
     Individualism and the American Dream in the Eighteenth
     Century." Ph.D. dissertation, University of Minnesota.
       Crèvecoeur's "agrarian-environmentalistic theory": na-
     ture is the source of the farmer's virtue; the farmer is a
     sociable entrepreneur and a conformist. Until the Revolu-
     tion, Crèvecoeur saw the middle colonies as the American
     utopia. In later life, Crèvecoeur showed conservative
     sympathies: he put economic individualism before the in-
     dividuality of thinking and acting for oneself.

1969

2   RAPPING, ELAYNE. "Harmonic Patchwork: The Art of Hector St.
       John de Crèvecoeur." Ph.D. dissertation, University of
       Pittsburgh.
          Both Letters and Voyage belong to the tradition of nar-
       rative prose fiction (the traveler's tale and imaginary
       voyage). Distinguishes between the "hero as traveler"
       (the "outward journey") and the "hero as narrator" (the
       "inward journey" of "mental development"). Letters ends
       "as an ironic satire or parody of itself, in which the
       central character and the basic structure are both exposed
       as artificial literary conventions...." Voyage presents
       many models (personal, historical, and metaphysical world
       views), and dramatizes the process by which these models
       are created and transformed.

1969 B SHORTER WRITINGS

1   BABUSCIO, JACK. "Crèvecoeur in Charles Town: The Negro in
       the Cage," Journal of Historical Studies, II, 283-86.
          Crèvecoeur deemphasizes the difficulties of regeneration,
       believing the ideal external environment will change the
       inner man. For Crèvecoeur, the "natural man" needs pro-
       tection from social pressures that would hinder self-
       reliance. The incident of the Negro in the cage shows
       Crèvecoeur "shocked into recognition of the tension" between
       reality and the ideal.

2   DAVIS, RICHARD B. "Hector St. John de Crèvecoeur," in Ameri-
       can Literature through Bryant, 1585-1830. New York:
       Appleton-Century-Crofts, pp. 64-65.
          Selected list of editions (exclusive of eighteenth-
       century ones), biographical and critical books and essays.

3   NYE, RUSSEL B. "Michel-Guillaume St. Jean de Crèvecoeur:
       Letters from an American Farmer," in Landmarks of American
       Writing, edited by Hennig Cohen. New York: Basic Books,
       pp. 32-45.
          Analysis and summary of each of the twelve letters--with
       special reference to the "two myths" of America as "Para-
       dise" and "Hope." Letters shows the American dream as
       more dream than reality. The book is an early landmark in
       the American literary tradition because of the following:
       (1) Crèvecoeur sees America "directly, through non-European
       eyes"; (2) he presents "the original self-reliant, self-
       sufficient, independent Yankee"; (3) he shows the charac-
       teristic American tendency to self-analysis; (4) he explores
       "the central enduring problem of American life...bridging
       the gap between America as fact and America as ideal."

1970 A BOOKS

1   PHILBRICK, THOMAS. St. John de Crèvecoeur. New York: Twayne
    Publishers.
        A critical biography. Crèvecoeur's works express "ex-
    traordinary awareness of the opposing forces" in man and
    nature. Chapters on the following: Crèvecoeur's life
    (with emphasis on his multiple identities); Letters as an
    expression of "the major items of the national faith";
    Letters as a "novel in embryo" (telling the story of
    James's movement toward disillusion) and composed of
    literary forms such as anecdote, confession, the symbolic
    scene; the new forms and "painterly quality" of Sketches;
    the French writings; Crèvecoeur's reputation. Praises
    Crèvecoeur's "complex artistry."

1970 B SHORTER WRITINGS

1   LEARY, LEWIS. "Crèvecoeur, J. Hector St. John," in Articles
    on American Literature, 1950-1967. Durham, N.C.: Duke
    University Press, p. 98.
        Lists journal articles on Crèvecoeur from 1950-1967.

2   MOHR, JAMES C. "Calculated Disillusionment: Crèvecoeur's
    Letters Reconsidered," SAQ, LXIX (Summer), 354-63.
        The simplistic view of Crèvecoeur as optimist ignores
    the "methodology" of the Letters. The ideal image of
    America presented in the first eight letters "becomes the
    dream against which the intensity of late disillusionment
    is measured." By letter twelve, the American Farmer knows
    he is seeking "an impossible dream." Crèvecoeur defines
    the American experience as "willingness to carry forward
    the ideals of civilization in the face of almost certain
    disillusionment."

3   NYE, RUSSEL B. "Aristocrat in the Forest: Crèvecoeur," in
    American Literary History: 1607-1830. New York: Alfred
    A. Knopf, pp. 154-59.
        Letter three is Crèvecoeur's most important piece of
    writing. In it he gives his famous definition of the
    American, analyzes American regional differences ("recog-
    nizing for probably the first time the unique significance
    of the American frontier") and explains for the first time
    how Europeans were transformed into Americans.

1972

1972 A   BOOKS - NONE

1972 B   SHORTER WRITINGS

1   CHRISTADLER, MARTIN. "St. John de Crèvecoeurs Letters from
         an American Farmer und die Anfänge des Amerikanischen
         Romans," Geschichte und Fiktion: Amerikanische Prosa im
         19. Jahrhundert, edited by Alfred Weber and Hartmut
         Grandel. Göttingen: Vandenhoeck and Ruprecht, pp. 42-63.
           Letters employs the techniques of narrative fiction. The
         book reveals Crèvecoeur's shift from optimism to pessimism
         through three techniques: the "essayistic" first person
         becomes a narrative first person; the idyllic opening
         gives way to the war; symbol and allegory reveal the
         multiple possibilities of America. Crèvecoeur's black/
         white oppositions tend to melodrama. The narrator's move-
         ment to despair suggests a popular American form, the
         initiation story. Hence Crèvecoeur anticipated later
         writers who show the American Adam in the romance.

1973 A   BOOKS - NONE

1973 B   SHORTER WRITINGS

1   LARSON, DAVID M. "Michel-Guillaume Jean de Crèvecoeur, Im-
         ported Enthusiasm," in "The Man of Feeling in America: A
         Study of Major Early American Writers' Attitudes Toward
         Benevolent Ethics and Behavior." Ph.D. dissertation, Uni-
         versity of Minnesota, pp. 176-232.
           Surveys the debates on Crèvecoeur. Some critics see him
         as realist or disillusioned cynic; others as sentimental
         "romanticist" who painted optimistic idylls. Actually,
         Crèvecoeur presents a bewildering variety of (sometimes
         contradictory) attitudes toward man, nature, and society,
         and does not try to reconcile these views. But his works
         are unified by a "consistent sensibility." "In almost all
         of his works, Crèvecoeur appears as a man of feeling par
         excellence": an "optimistic celebrant of the pleasures of
         existence," a "sentimental misanthrope," or an "aesthetic
         relisher of others' distresses."

1974

.974 A   BOOKS - NONE

.974 B   SHORTER WRITINGS

SPILLER, ROBERT E., et al., eds. "(Michel-Guillaume Jean)
St. Jean de Crèvecoeur, 1735-1813," in Literary History of
the United States: Bibliography. 4th ed., revised.
New York: Macmillan Co., pp. 461-62, 896, 1174-75.
   Selected bibliography of editions of Crèvecoeur's works,
reprints, biography and criticism.

Index

Codes refer to the respective sections of the text.
JB=John Bartram; WB=William Bartram; B=Byrd; C=Crèvecoeur

Abbott, Elizabeth O., JB1904.B1;
  JB1907.B1; JB1915.B1
Account of East-Florida, with a
  Journal, Kept by John
  Bartram of Philadelphia,
  Botanist to His Majesty for
  the Floridas; upon a Jour-
  ney from St. Augustine up
  the River St. John's, An,
  "The Introduction" to,
  JB1767.B2
"Account of the Bartram Garden,"
  JB1864.B1
"Account of the Bartram Garden,
  Philadelphia, An,"
  JB1929.B1
Adams, Percy G., B1956.B1;
  B1967.B1; C1946.A1;
  C1947.B1; C1948.B1;
  C1949.B1; C1953.B1;
  C1961.B1; C1962.B1
Addison. See Augustans
Agee, William H., C1969.A1
Agrarianism, Crèvecoeur and,
  C1916.A1; C1947.B2;
  C1949.B2; C1964.B2;
  C1967.B1; C1969.A1
Allen, J. A., WB1876.B1-B2
[Allibone, Samuel A.],
  JB1859.B1; WB1859.B1
"Alligators of the Okefinokee,"
  WB1930.B1
America and Her Commentators:
  With a Critical Sketch of
  Travel in the United
  States, JB1864.B2; WB1864.B1

American Book Collectors and
  Collecting from Colonial
  Times to the Present,
  "William Byrd II of West-
  over," B1941.B1
"American Botanical Gardens and
  English Poetry," WB1928.B1
American dream, the, in Crève-
  coeur's works. See Optimism
  in Crèvecoeur's works
"American-English Communications
  of Three Colonial Scholars,
  1700-1775," JB1932.B1
"American Farmer Returns, The,"
  C1925.B5
"'American Farmer' St. John de
  Crèvecoeur and His Famous
  'Letters' (1735-1813), The,"
  C1906.B2
"American Farmer's Letters, With
  a Check-list of the Differ-
  ent Editions, The,"
  C1934.B1
"American Indian in English
  Literature of the Eighteenth
  Century, The," WB1925.B1;
  C1925.B1
American Literature through
  Bryant, 1585-1830: "John
  Bartram (1700?-1768),"
  JB1969.B1; "William Bartram
  (1739-1823)," WB1969.B2;
  "William Byrd (1674-1744),"
  B1969.B2; "Hector St. John
  de Crèvecoeur," C1969.B2

153

Exportation of plants to England.
See Collinson, Peter;
Bartram, John: as botanist,
correspondence of
Expression in America, "Be-
ginnings," C1932.B1
"Extract of Mr. Wm. [sic]
Bartram's Observations in
a Journey up the River
Savannah in Georgia with
His Son, on Discoveries,
An," JB1767.B1
"Extraits. Belles-lettres,"
C1787.B2
"Eye Witnesses to a Vanished
America," JB1956.B1;
WB1956.B1

Fagin, N. Bryllion, WB1931.B3;
WB1933.A1; WB1939.B2
Fairchild, Howie N., C1961.B3
Fairs, John T., JB1928.B3
Farmer's Register, The, B1839.B1;
B1841.B2-B3; "Editor's
Preface" in, B1841.B1
"Fasti Ornithologiae Redivivi--
No. I. Bartram's Travels,"
WB1875.B1
Fäy, Bernard, C1925.B7
"Finishing Stroke to Bartram,
The," WB1899.B1
First Century of American
Literature: 1770-1870,
The, B1935.B2; "The
Emerging West" in, C1935.B1
Fishwick, Marshall, B1959.B1
"Florida," JB1827.B1; WB1827.B1
"Foreign Literature, Article I,"
C1801.B2
"Foreign Notices: North
America. Bartram's Botanic
Garden on the Schuylkill,
near Philadelphia,"
JB1832.B1
Fothergill, Dr. John, WB1919.B2;
WB1944.B1. See also
Bartram, William, biography
Fox, Frank, WB1967.B1
Fox, Richard Hingston, JB1915.B3;
JB1919.B1; WB1919.B2

Franklinia alatamaha ("Franklin
tree"), JB1928.B4;
JB1933.B1; JB1936.B1;
JB1937.B1; WB1928.B6;
WB1933.B1; WB1937.B1
"Franklin and Crèvecoeur: Indi-
vidualism and the American
Dream in the Eighteenth
Century," C1969.A1
Franklin, Benjamin, C1947.B1;
C1962.B1
"Freehold Concept in Eighteenth
Century American Letters,
The," C1947.B2
"From 'Kubla Khan' to Florida,"
WB1956.B2
Frontier, Byrd and the, B1927.B4;
B1928.B1; B1929.B1;
B1937.B1; B1939.B2;
B1955.B1; B1959.B2;
B1971.A1; B1972.B2
"Frontier: Lubberland, The,"
B1927.B4

Gabriel, Ralph H., C1925.B8
Garden and Forest, JB1889.B1-B3
Gee, Wilson, WB1918.B2
"Genealogical Chart of the
Bunting Family," JB1895.B1
"Geschichte. Paris, bey Cuchet:
Lettres d'un Cultivateur
Américain," C1785.B3
"Glance at Wordsworth's Reading,
A," WB1915.B1
Götze, August E., C1788.B7
"Grand Planteur Virginien au
XVIIIe Siècle: William
Byrd de Westover, Un,"
B1964.B2
Great American Gentleman,
William Byrd of Westover
in Virginia (His Secret
Diary for the Years 1709-
1712), The, "Introduction"
to, B1963.B2
Green Laurels: The Lives and
Achievements of the Great
Naturalists, JB1936.B1
Gummere, Richard M., WB1955.B1;
B1964.B1